SCHOOL AND COLLEGE

A CARNEGIE FOUNDATION SPECIAL REPORT

School and College

PARTNERSHIPS IN EDUCATION

GENE I. MAEROFF

WITH A FOREWORD BY

ERNEST L. BOYER

THE CARNEGIE FOUNDATION FOR THE

ADVANCEMENT OF TEACHING

5 IVY LANE, PRINCETON, NEW JERSEY, 08540

Fourth printing, 1986

ISBN 0-931050-22-7

LC 83-70359

Copies are available from the
PRINCETON UNIVERSITY PRESS
3175 Princeton Pike
Lawrenceville, N.J. 08648

CONTENTS

FOREWORD

by Ernest L. Boyer

WITH THIS PUBLICATION, The Carnegie Foundation for the Advancement of Teaching inaugurates a new series of *special reports*. Our expectation is that these publications will focus on issues of special challenges and concerns, ones that grow out of large scale foundation studies.

School and College is a case in point. This special report reflects a longstanding interest of our Foundation in what is often referred to as the "seamless web" of education. The subject of school-college collaboration has been of concern to us from almost the beginning, and it relates to our current study of the American high school that will be released later this year.

Last year The Carnegie Foundation helped to organize the nation's first national conference of state school superintendents and college and university presidents. That meeting proved eminently successful and I am pleased that this report on the school-college partnership will be released at the second such gathering—this time at Yale University in 1983.

Our hope is that this publication and the meetings that bring school and college officials together will help to close the gap that is increasingly intolerable if American education is to progress and fulfill its promise. Education involves many relationships at many different levels, and, in the end, all of these linkages must be strong. If they are not, the chain will snap and the nation will suffer an unbearable loss of education effectiveness.

Gene Maeroff, an education writer for *The New York Times* and author of the recent well-regarded book, *Don't Blame the Kids*, was an obvious choice for the task of preparing this special report.

Drawing upon his own knowledge and rich experience, Maeroff has been able to identify a remarkable variety of school and college partnerships. The report is not intended to be exhaustive, but rather illustrative of the great diversity of partnership activities now in progress. We are pleased to have joined with Mr. Maeroff in preparing this report on some of the significant programs that strengthen the linkages between the nation's colleges and schools.

These are tough times for American education. Enrollments are declining, budgets have been cut, federal mandates have sharply shifted and public confidence in education has weakened. Some colleges and schools will be able to ride out the storm, continuing their journey in splendid isolation. For most, however, there is an unmistakable mandate: join together and make the trip more successful for the institution and rewarding to the students.

Gene Maeroff's coast-to-coast survey reveals a dramatic upsurge in collaboration. Colleges and schools have come together to accomplish clear, explicit goals, objectives that should be pursued by every institution in every state.

The lessons to be learned from this report are clear. First, high schools and colleges should join together to determine the content and specific skills considered essential requirements for entrance into college.

Second, colleges and schools should work together to overcome the tyranny of time. Students should be free to move at their own pace, more flexibly to make the transition from school to college.

Third, our programs for beginning teachers and for senior teachers should be collaboratively developed by colleges and schools.

Fourth, experimental transition schools should be established that combine the school-college years and avoid curricular overlap and duplication.

Fifth, collaboration is urgently required to identify disadvantaged students at an early age and provide constantly the help they require as they move from school to college.

Sixth, every college and university should establish a partnership with one or more school districts to provide educational and cultural enrichment as determined by principals and teachers at the schools.

Today, nearly one out of every two high school graduates goes directly into higher education. A closer relationship between the two levels of education is urgently required. The sampling of programs surveyed in this report is only the top of an iceberg of a massive and rapidly expanding movement in the nation as schools and colleges focus increasingly not on the bureaucracy but on students.

A word of caution: Projects reviewed in the report show little evidence of evaluation. Teachers get some training, students get a chance to accelerate their education, a school and college share facilities. In few instances is there any formal documentation that the change has made an enduring difference. Evidence is needed to show that cooperation is worth the money and effort. Besides validating what has occurred, this may persuade other schools and colleges to follow suit.

This is not an easy challenge to meet. Money for collaborative projects is scarce, and every dollar diverted to evaluation will be that much less to be spent in behalf of the program itself. Also, there is the difficulty of assessing whether a student benefits in the long-run, for example, from having been taught by a teacher who was helped by a college professor in preparing the course. Yet, advocates of closer cooperation ought to have some concern about proving the worth of their projects.

Further, with all the talk about togetherness, the power of tradition remains strong. There is no particular reason, for example, why four years of high school and four years of college is the most desirable combination for producing an educated person. What about three years of high school and five years of college? Or five years of high school and three years of college? Or four years of high school and five years of college, as is routine for some students pursuing degrees in engineering or architecture.

Too often, the last year seems like it ought not to count. It is a time when students in high school feel they are no longer part of one world and have not yet passed into the next world. Surely, schools and colleges could create a more satisfactory transition period that blends the two levels in a way that carries the student forward more smoothly and enhances, and does not detract from the purposes of education.

Though the lockstep has loosened a bit, the patterns of the past remain entrenched. Even with a year off between high school and college, or a brief stopping-out from college, the immutable four-four combination continues intact. Society pays homage to habit, and, in education, habits are perhaps most pervasive. The rhythm of the academic pattern stirs the soul for a lifetime; people have trouble envisioning education in any form other than that which it has always taken.

Years after they have left school and college, people continue to feel that the onset of autumn is when all things begin anew. Never mind that nature's resurgence is in the spring and the planting cycle is drawing to a close in September.

These ties to tradition are not easily severed. Significant reform requires conviction—not tea and cookies in the afternoon.

Finally, the potential for cooperation between schools and colleges can be no greater than the ability to agree on common goals. As it is, objectives sometimes seem subject to whim. What is it that schools and colleges, working together, expect of their graduates? What do they want to achieve through their collaboration? Some educators seem content to respond to the demand of the moment. A fickle nation that has rushed to worship at the altar of computer literacy appears to have readily abandoned its earlier faith in other kinds of literacy. Quieter voices that still whisper of the need for mastery of written language have been drowned out by the latest round of hosannas for technology.

Efforts to improve cooperation will remain hit-or-miss ventures, outside the mainstream, so long as the objectives of the eight years of high school and college remain unclarified. Experiments come and go, projects die and new ones are born. But there is no sense of continuity. There is no agreement on appropriate curriculum at either level. Lip service is paid to the value of a general education but those who fashion the curriculum cannot resist flirting with careerism.

Perhaps some stability will result from the unprecedented scrutiny of the American high school that is under way. From out of this reexamination may emerge a new sense of what high school ought to be and how it fits into the education that follows.

Collaboration is not an automatic virtue. Not every cooperative venture is destined for success. But to those who make the effort and occasionally succeed, the rewards are high and students are well served. There can be no better reason for working together.

CHAPTER I

Partnership for Excellence

IT HAPPENED IN the late 1970s during one of those rituals when the presidents of Ohio's state-supported universities are summoned before a legislative committee to defend their budgets. Several of them were there—Harold L. Enarson, the now retired president of Ohio State University, the late Hollis A. Moore, president of Bowling Green State University, and others. "All of us were lined up like so many blackbirds on a fence, each carrying one of those big books filled with numbers," recalled Enarson. "Then the steady drumfire began. 'Why,' they wanted to know, 'were the universities asking the State of Ohio to pay twice for the same thing? Why all this money for remediation after the high schools had already been paid to teach the same material?' "[1]

And so it has gone all across the country as the problems of the high schools have reminded everyone of the connection between what happens to students before they get to college and after they arrive on campus.

Until very recently, school districts have had to fend for themselves, struggling to bring order out of educational confusion, unable to persuade students to enroll in courses that the young people knew they no longer needed to gain admission to college, caught in the cross-fire of conflicting goals.

Institutions of higher education have remained aloof. Aside from the obvious role of preparing the men and women who teach in elementary and secondary schools, colleges and universities have been reluctant to enter into partnerships designed to enhance cooperation between the two sectors. In many cases, high schools have been left without any sense of what the colleges expect graduates to know.

Recently, the relationship has begun to change. Representatives of higher education and the public schools are taking notice of each other, with and without the prodding of legislators. Discussion of mutual problems has begun, and there is tacit acknowledgement that it is time to overcome the distrust that has proved so obdurate a barrier to cooperation.

Perhaps it took the shock treatment of remediation—having to offer college courses built around high school level content—to hasten the change in mood. Perhaps it was the loss in public confidence in education at all levels. Or the downturn in enrollments may have been what finally jolted higher education into a state of receptiveness. In any event, college and school educators are showing more interest in each other. Conferences, conversations, and collaborative projects are cropping up from coast to coast.

There is ample precedent for such partnerships. The roots of cooperation stretch to the early 19th century, when teacher-training institutions actually organized their own lower schools so incipient teachers would have a place to practice what they were learning. Those institutions felt a vested interest in early education that few colleges or universities today recognize. Just as public education was born in Massachusetts, so were the normal schools and, eventually, the practice schools or *laboratory* schools—as they were later called—that were adjuncts of those normal schools.

In 1900, The College Entrance Examination Board was organized to standardize the academic requirements for college, propose subject area tests in English, mathematics, and history and make more orderly the transition to postsecondary education.

After Sputnik togetherness flourished once again, new curricula in biology, physics, English, and mathematics were prepared. Schools and colleges, together, pushed for excellence in education.

The relationship was at times unhealthy. Colleges would often take the schools for granted. In paternalistic fashion, curricula would be packaged and teacher training programs planned with little or no consultation with the schools. Still, an effort was made to break out of the layer-cake approach to education.

During the 1960s, cooperation came to a screeching halt. New priorities came crashing in. Colleges and universities were caught up in the free speech movement, marches, sit-ins, teach-ins and other protests over Cambodia and Kent State.

The civil rights movement pushed colleges to expand educational opportunity for minorities and women, and school districts were preoccupied with compensatory education and the challenge of desegregation. Concerns about academic excellence, curriculum continuity, and school-college collaboration were forgotten.

Like lapsed lovers who had more important things to do, high schools and colleges stopped communicating with each other. They complained in each case that their efforts were unappreciated by the other.

High schools imitated colleges and universities in fragmenting the curriculum and stuffing it full of electives. Left on their own, too many high school students failed to take the courses that would best prepare them to get the most out of college. In its peculiar way, justice prevailed, with institutions of higher education being forced to mount remedial courses for these same students. There is no telling how much of this tragedy might have been averted.

Finally, however, there is a reconciliation. Conversation has resumed, and the two parties are acting cordially, though not quite ready to climb back into bed together.

This special Carnegie report describes school-college collaboration from coast to coast. It is not an exhaustive inventory of all the splendid projects now in progress. Instead, it presents selected case studies. From these successful programs, five basic principles emerge that must be followed if collaborative projects are to succeed.

First, to achieve effective school-college cooperation, educators at both levels must agree that they, indeed, have common problems. This point is embarrassingly obvious—it's like Knute Rockne telling his players that first they need a football. Yet the harsh truth is that many educators are convinced that they can go it all alone. It is reported that Henry David Thoreau scorned the idea of stringing telegraph lines between Maine and Texas because he wondered what in the world New Englanders and Texans could possibly have to say to one another![2] Today, many school and college people are like Texans and New Englanders before the telegraph. They have no messages to send, or so they think. And yet education is a seamless web; communication between the sectors is urgently required.

Second, in order to achieve effective collaboration, the traditional academic "pecking order" must be overcome. Colleges and universities have had—for many years—a "plantation mentality" about the schools.

Higher education set the ground rules and the schools were expected passively to go along.

Consider, for example, the way college admission requirements are established and abandoned. Faculty committees deliberate in splendid isolation. They make decisions that have enormous impact on the school curriculum. Yet, when these dramatic moves are made, teachers, principals, and superintendents rarely are consulted.

Consider also, the way continuing education programs are unilaterally developed. All too often, schools of education decide what courses should be taught and when they should be taught. Frequently the "real needs" of teachers are not adequately considered.

Fortunately, this traditional pecking order is beginning to break down. But even in the case studies in this report, time and time again, so-called "cooperative" programs were launched with very little consultation with the schools.

The point is this. If the quality of American education is to succeed, "top-down" planning will not do. Teachers and administrators in the public schools must be full partners in the process.

Third, if school-college collaboration is to succeed, cooperative projects must be sharply focused.

Recently, a school-college project was announced in a midwestern city. With great enthusiasm, everyone had agreed to work together. Greetings were exchanged, everyone was toasted, but it soon became clear that everyone was completely vague about the *specific* problem they hoped collaboratively to solve.

To put it very simply, school-college "togetherness" must be something more than an academic love-in. Serious cooperation will occur only if school and college people agree to focus on *one* or *two* specific goals and work to keep programs sharply focused. You simply cannot do everything at once.

Fourth, it seems quite clear that if school-college cooperation is to be successful, those who participate must get recognition. Collaboration will win or lose to the degree that participants understand that the projects are important and that there will be professional rewards.

Consider *Project Advance* at Syracuse University which is described in Chapter 3. Through this program, 4,000 high school seniors in 77 high

4

schools in New York, New Jersey, Massachusetts, and Michigan currently are taking, in the high school, transferable college credit courses in biology, calculus, chemistry, English, psychology, religion, and sociology. These courses are taught by high school teachers trained by Syracuse University, and they are supervised by professors of appropriate departments.

Project Advance has been a great success because it is a true partnership and because the project is sharply focused. But the program *also* is a success because teachers are *rewarded*. High schools pay a stipend for teachers to participate in the Syracuse summer training program, which is viewed as professional development. Instructional materials are furnished by the University.

Teachers are given the title of Syracuse "Adjunct Instructor," which makes them eligible for scholarship grants at the University, or, in some cases, at other institutions close to home. Participating teachers also may receive 50 percent of the cost of graduate credits (for a masters or Ph.D.). And those participating are recognized, within their schools and communities, as outstanding teachers.

The fifth commandment is equally important: For school-college cooperation to work, it must focus on action—not machinery.

Time and time again, when people think about collaboration they focus first on budgets and bureaucracy, on the costs involved, on hiring one or two directors, on renting space, and on such high priority items as paper clips and a new letterhead.

This, of course, is self-defeating. And, quite frankly, this kind of talk frequently is a smokescreen for an unwillingness to act. While resources are important, they should not become the preoccupation of school and college planners.

Time and time again, the most successful programs are those where people see a need and find time to act with little red tape or extra funding.

Here then is the conclusion. Cooperation among the nation's colleges and schools is absolutely urgent. But if we are to succeed:
• A common agenda must be acknowledged.
• A true spirit of collaboration must emerge.
• A single project must be identified.
• Those involved must be adequately rewarded.
• The focus must be on activities, not machinery.

The following chapters present a series of school-college projects that illustrate many of the five essential ingredients just described. In the projects, schools and colleges are working together to establish standards, accelerate students' progress, create new kinds of institutions, educate teachers, and enrich the schools. The goal in all of these examples is to serve the student, not the system.

In 1750, Benjamin Franklin wrote to Samuel Johnson as follows: "I think, with you, that nothing is of more importance for the public good, than to form and train up youth in wisdom (and) in virtue." Franklin went on to say that "Wise and good men are, in my opinion, the strength of the state. Much more so than riches or arms which, under the monument of ignorance and wickedness often draw destruction instead of providing safety for the people."[3]

And at this moment, as national priorities are being aggressively reexamined, the nation's colleges and schools should come together to reaffirm the conviction of Ben Franklin that, in the end, nothing is more important to the public good than the training up of the youth.

CHAPTER II

Setting Standards

"THE HIGH SCHOOLS in this country are always at the mercy of the colleges," said A. Bartlett Giamatti, the president of Yale University. "The colleges change their requirements and their admissions criteria, and the high schools, by which I mean public and private parochial schools, are constantly trying to catch up with what the colleges are thinking. When the colleges don't seem to know what they think over a period of time, it's no wonder that this oscillation takes place all the way through 'the system.' "[1]

In the fall of 1982, about 1.5 million students, roughly half of all students who graduated from high school, went on to some form of post-secondary education. What determines if a high school student can go on to college? About one-fourth of all institutions accept every high school graduate who applies. Most frequent at community colleges, this policy is also found at about 20 percent of all four-year public colleges. About one-half (56 percent) of all colleges admit all who meet minimum standards—the completion of high school with a *C* average and a minimum score on the admission test. At the colleges, about three out of four students who take the test meet the requirement.[2]

The fact is that across the board, not just at community colleges, college entrance requirements place little, and in some cases *no*, emphasis on the substantive content of what high school students should have mastered as the necessary prerequisite to college study. There is no common body of knowledge, no specific set of intellectual skills against which students can measure their own readiness or on which colleges can base admission and placement decisions.

At those colleges that do require more than this, a student's standing in the high school class is by far the most important factor. On the other hand, fewer than half of all institutions consider test scores to be important. Many private four-year colleges still use test scores to confirm a student's record of performance in high school. Only 2 percent of all institutions consider the admission test score to be the most important factor in determining admission.

Surprisingly, the courses a student takes are not important in getting into most colleges, although they may be critical to success once a student is there. Half the colleges set *no* specific course requirements at all, and only about one-fourth consider courses the students took in making the decision for or against admission. When specific courses *are* identified, the most frequently required courses are English (the usual requirement being four years), mathematics (two years is the average requirement) and the physical sciences (one year).

Simply stated, admission decisions relate only indirectly to the content of the high school experience or to mastery of specific fields of knowledge. Young people and the high schools know this. Colleges have sidestepped the content of education in their admission decisions. This, in turn, leaves high schools and young people with only vague notions about what an adequate education is all about and how they can best prepare for college.

The paradox is that while colleges and universities had dropped their standards and found it impossible to agree on the meaning of a college education, they continued to take potshots at the schools. "The high schools were getting a bad rap in many ways," said Michael Kirst, a professor at Stanford and a former president of the California State Board of Education. "The colleges were sitting up there in splendid isolation talking about the deficiencies of entering students, and not doing anything about it."

A glance at what happened to foreign and classical languages in the high schools during the 1970s shows how the steadily shifting college requirements lowered the underpinnings of the high school curriculum. When youngsters discovered they no longer needed to study a foreign language to get into college or to get out of college they deserted the courses. By 1978, about 15 percent of the nation's secondary school students, less than half the percentage of 1915, were enrolled in a foreign language according to the President's Commission of Foreign Languages. Furthermore, 6 out of 10 of those in the 15 percent were in first-year courses and chances were they would pursue their foreign language study no further.[3]

"I don't blame the colleges alone for the drop in standards," said Scott Thompson, executive director of the National Association of Secondary School Principals in an interview. "It was a broad, society-wide shift in emphasis. But the colleges played a part in it. Right now, the colleges are genuine in their feelings that too many students are not adequately prepared for higher education. On the other hand, if the colleges had a modicum of conscience they must know that their own shift in standards and requirements had something to do with the situation that faces the schools today."

By the early 1980s, there were some very definite efforts under way to let high school students know what would be expected of them. Admission requirements were being changed or reviewed for the public systems of higher education in 27 states, according to a survey in 1982 by the National Association of Secondary School Principals.[4] In most cases, there was the demand that high school students spend more years studying specific courses. Additionally, higher admission test scores were mandated, class rank requirements were upgraded, and higher grade point averages were established.

There is much more to the connection between higher education and precollegiate education, however, than the setting of standards to which high school students are expected to adhere. In fact, there is some danger of higher education becoming dictatorial. Like all pendulums, this one apparently must swing to the extreme before gliding back to the middle. This is part of the reaction to the years of inattention during which colleges and universities cared little about the ways they influenced the prior preparation of their students.

After all, it is not easy to overcome the effects of having allowed the curriculum to be transformed into a smorgasbord of electives, often more tasty than nutritious. It was a period when courses were treated like light bulbs, interchangeable, even though some burned with the brilliance of 500 watts and others barely cast a glow into the corridors of intellect.

The confrontation between the college presidents and the legislators in Ohio gave birth to a fresh attempt to have the publicly-supported colleges and universities use their influence to raise the level of preparation in the high schools. Though the State Capitol in Columbus is linked to the Ohio State campus by High Street, the lawmakers traditionally have been interested in the connection only on Saturday afternoons in the fall, when their clout has helped them obtain comfortable seats on the 50-yard line to watch the powerful Buckeyes crush Iowa, Minnesota, or some other erstwhile foe.

But the climate has changed, and by the late 1970s the clouds of possible legislative action hovered over Ohio State and many other state-sponsored campuses. This threat got educators in Ohio to reexamine the relationship between secondary schools and higher education. What had long been taken for granted was a subject for scrutiny. The State Board of Education and the Ohio Board of Regents formed an advisory commission to study the issues and to offer recommendations.

In Ohio, the law requires that "a graduate of the twelfth grade shall be entitled to admission without examination to any college or university which is supported wholly or in part by the state." Higher education is dependent on the quality of preparation in the secondary schools. The state universities do not have the luxury of weeding out and refusing admission to students they deem incapable of doing the work.

State-sponsored colleges and universities in Ohio, as well as those in other open-admissions states, are not likely to have better prepared freshmen unless they are allowed to say more about the earlier education of those students. This means, of course, evincing some concern about the quality of teaching and learning in the elementary and secondary schools.

The advisory commission in Ohio quickly concluded that there was a need to strengthen the English and mathematics courses given to students in high schools across the state. But the panel also saw that the existence of better courses would not make a difference unless more students enrolled in such courses. The pitifully low enrollments in Latin classes in many high schools during the 1970s, for instance, showed that simply offering a course was not enough to raise standards. As it was, youngsters knew that they could get admitted to a state university regardless of what courses they took, just so they obtained a diploma. Finally, the advisory commission recognized that trying to offer better courses implied a need for teachers qualified to teach such courses.

This was the problem, and the advisory commission sought to solve it without destroying the carefully nurtured equality of opportunity that open admissions had provided in Ohio. "While we need to refocus attention . . . this does not require a lesser commitment to education for a heterogeneous and pluralistic population," the commission warned in its final report in 1981.[5]

It recommended that the college preparatory curriculum in every high school in Ohio include four years of English and at least three years of mathematics. Moreover, it recommended that every private and state-sponsored four-year college and university in Ohio require that students take these courses in order to gain unconditional admission.

Viewed as crucial to all this was the need to provide good teachers. "How the teacher is prepared and kept current in fulfilling this responsibility is critical in formulating course components for high school students," the commission stated.[6] Thus, the group recommended that teacher certification requirements reflect a greater emphasis on subject matter in the content areas. As more and more states are discovering, methodology alone is not sufficient to make good teachers.

What was so stunning about all this was that, for the first time, the State of Ohio was telling students they no longer would be unconditionally admitted to college. Open admissions was not abrogated, but suddenly students had an obligation to show that they had tried to prepare themselves to a minimum level as their part of the agreement for maintaining the open door policy. Each college and university in Ohio is free to adopt the recommendations as it sees fit.

One of the first to make this move was Kent State University, which welcomed the opportunity to combat the high attrition that had prevented so many of its freshmen from completing their degrees. Starting in the fall of 1983, applicants to Kent will have to demonstrate better preparation—the minimum number years prescribed by the advisory commission in each high school subject—to gain unconditional admission to the university. The only other way to be unconditionally admitted to Kent will be for an applicant to have at least a C-plus average and a minimum score of 19 on the American College Testing program examination. Everyone else will be admitted conditionally, required to appear on campus before the beginning of the academic year to take a battery of placement tests for possible assignment to remedial courses.

"We hope that by doing all this," said Michael Schwartz, who moved up from provost to president of Kent in 1982, "we will give high schools more muscle with the college-bound students and that the students will take the courses that best prepare them for college."[7]

In Florida, the Postsecondary Education Planning Commission recently called for a detailed definition of the college curriculum, particularly in the first two years. This is viewed as a prerequisite to defining what the schools should be expected to provide as preparation for college study. The Commission calls for the phase-out of all remedial education at the college level by 1988, with that responsibility to be totally assumed by the high schools.

In New Jersey, all freshmen entering public colleges and universities are tested in basic skills. Of the approximately 30,000 students who took the tests in 1981, only 38 percent were fully proficient in computation at a *sixth grade level*, and 35 percent failed to demonstrate competence at this minimal level. Most discouraging of all, even the 7,000 students who had taken college preparatory courses in mathematics—algebra, geometry, and advanced algebra—did poorly. Only 4 percent of these were judged fully proficient in algebra and nearly two-thirds failed that portion of the test. Results for the test of verbal skills were hardly more encouraging. Of all the students who took the tests, 28 percent were rated as proficient, about 44 percent were lacking in one area (reading, vocabulary, grammar, writing) or another, and 28 percent failed in all areas.[8]

The colleges are not allowed to admit students who score poorly unless adequate remedial programs are provided. Information on students' performance on the tests is sent back to their high schools and is also made available to the press.

On the West Coast, the California Round Table on Educational opportunity has brought together the state's top education officials. "Colleges and universities bear major responsibility for efforts to improve secondary education," the Round Table asserted as its working thesis.[9] The linchpin of the Round Table's efforts is an attempt to achieve common understanding of the content of instruction at each level of schooling and to build up college and university entrance requirements, hoping that this, in turn, will help the high schools raise their standards.

The academic senates of the California Community Colleges, the California State University, and the University of California recommended

12

that every student planning to pursue a bachelor's degree take at least four years of English and at least three years of mathematics in high school. Moreover, at least one course in each of these subjects should be taken in the senior year, which had disintegrated into an academic wasteland for many students in California high schools. The voluminous statement prepared by the academic senates includes lengthy descriptions of the kinds of skills that students should acquire in each subject and samples of the sort of work they should be able to handle.

In Utah, a full-page advertisement appearing in *The Salt Lake Tribune* just a year ago said it all. Addressed to high school students and their parents as an open letter from the University of Utah, the advertisement listed a recommended course of study in high school that purportedly would increase chances for success at the institution. "Failure to complete these courses will diminish the probability of success and most likely extend the period of time needed to obtain a degree," was the warning.[10]

Beginning in 1987, it was recommended that students have two years of mathematics even though only one was required; three years of science even though only two were required; four years of history and social studies, even though only one was required; three years of foreign language, even though only two were required; and two years of fine arts, even though no such courses were required. Four years of English would be required of all.

In this way, the University of Utah, an institution with a long commitment to the principle of open admissions, was telling its prospective students that they were still entitled to a higher education, but that if they were serious about it, they had better be properly prepared. Grade point average was not the issue; the university simply wanted the students to take the right courses, however well or poorly they did.

As if the message needed amplification, Utah announced that there would be no more remedial courses offered as part of the regular program on campus after the middle 1980s. Students will have to take remedial courses at off-campus extension sites, paying extra and receiving no credit.

"The presence on campus of an increasing number of poorly or marginally prepared students accounts for the rise in the number of remedial offerings the university has been obliged to arrange and for the hindered rate of learning our average and more qualified students have been experiencing," said David Pierpont Gardner, president of the university.

"This trend, if left unchecked, and when coupled with the huge increases in enrollment that are predicted for the university beginning in the latter part of this decade, will prove to be the undoing of any effort we might make to sustain, much less to improve, the quality and rigor of our teaching programs and the national respect which we presently enjoy."[11]

Copies of the advertisement are pinned on the walls of advisors' offices in high schools from Logan to Cedar City, a not too subtle reminder that expectations are rising.

These moves to clarify standards for admission are in the right direction. But colleges should not act alone. If higher education officials dictate high-handedly what they want and run newspaper ads without the simple courtesy of consultation, resentment will understandably develop. As Patrick Callan, director of the California Postsecondary Education Commission, points out: "Constructive collaboration should replace the fruitless rhetorical exchange in which we attack the schools for the quality of the students they send us, and they respond by criticizing universities for the quality of teachers we send them."[12]

Clearly, all states should establish a school-college panel to permit educators at both levels to agree upon the core of education and develop a school-college curriculum that provides both continuity and coherence.

One final point. High schools are usually in the dark about how their students perform when they go off to college. The colleges pass along general complaints—or praise—but there is no specific information to let secondary schools know how their students measure up.

Every summer, North Carolina State University at Raleigh provides a student performance summary to each of the nearly 800 high schools from which the previous year's freshmen came. The performance of each student is reported relative to the entire freshman class. The report includes information such as SAT scores, mean high school grade point average, freshman year grade point average, and performance on freshman English, mathematics, and science courses. With concrete information such as this, the high school administrator knows how the school measures up.

It is not unreasonable to expect that every college and university not only establish clear and reasonable standards for admission but also report back to secondary schools regarding the academic performance of their graduates.

CHAPTER III

Accelerating Students

ARRY S. TRUMAN was in the White House and Dwight D. Eisenhower was still on Morningside Heights. In the United States Senate, a Tennessean named Kefauver was making himself famous by investigating organized crime. An iconoclastic preppy by the name of Caulfield had just been introduced to the nation's readers and South Pacific was the rage of the Great White Way. Bogey was waist-high in muck, trying to tug the African Queen through stagnant waters. It was 1951, and the entire enrollment in higher education was 2,302,000.

There also was a troublesome little war in an out-of-the-way Asian country known as Korea. Truman had just fired MacArthur and it appeared that the United States, a mere six years after the massive mobilizations of World War II, might be on the verge of universal military conscription of 18-year-olds. The presidents of some institutions of higher education thought that, if this were to happen, young people should have at least a couple of years of college before going off to do battle for their country. A way to do this would be to start admitting students as freshmen at the age of 16, without waiting for them to get high school diplomas.

For this reason, and others of a more purely educational nature, several institutions of higher education agreed to participate in the Program for Early Admission to College. The experiment, sponsored by the Fund for the Advancement of Education, an arm of the Ford Foundation, turned out to be one of the sledgehammers that finally broke the lockstep of educational inflexibility.

The 12 institutions that ultimately joined the program agreed to admit as freshmen some students who had completed only the tenth or eleventh grade of high school. It was a rudimentary effort to strengthen the bond between high schools and colleges, though the high schools were largely excluded from any policy-making role in the program. They were supposed to be happy just to provide the students. Nevertheless, the results were satisfactory and, in most cases, the early admittees rose to the challenge.

In 1957, reviewing the program, it was possible for the author of a report to observe: "Each child begins at age six and moves forward one grade each year until he emerges from high school 12 years later. Then he may march through four years of college, still in step with his chronological peers. This solution to the problem of educational logistics has many administrative advantages, but pressed toward its logical extreme it defeats our efforts to serve the individual capacities of children."[1]

Most importantly, the Program for Early Admission demonstrated that students progressing through the educational system did not have to be treated like grains of sand passing through the neck of an hourglass. Their speed could vary according to individual needs. Chronological age did not have to be a tyrannical yardstick for measuring readiness for college. Yet, it took the dislocation of war to make the point.

At about the same time that the Early Admission Program was being organized, another seminal effort was being launched to enable high school students to encounter college-level work before they were 18 years old. Twelve institutions of higher education and 12 high schools were joining forces to allow students to take courses on a college level in their high school classrooms. After successfully completing the courses and entering college, the students were to receive either academic credit or automatic placement in higher level courses or both. This was the origin of the Advanced Placement program that has since come under the sponsorship of the College Entrance Examination Board.

It is easy to take Advanced Placement for granted now, 30 years after the fateful gathering that spawned the program. But the differences that had to be overcome at the time were considerable and, in some ways, a reminder of the obstacles that still confront cooperative efforts. "The source of the difficulty appears to lie deeper, in the relative independence of school and college requirements," said the committee report that grew out of those early deliberations. "The basic weakness, in the judgment of many observers is a failure of the school and college to view their jobs as parts of a continuous process, two halves of a common enterprise."[2]

That statement made three decades ago could just as well have been

16

written yesterday. What has evolved is a program that is the largest of its kind in the country allowing high school students to pursue college-level work.

In May of 1982, 141,626 students from 5,525 high schools took 188,933 Advanced Placement examinations. Results were sent to 1,976 colleges and universities.[3] The examinations, prepared by the Educational Testing Service and given under the auspices of the College Board, are the common standard against which all students are measured—whether their course was taken in a small rural high school on a dusty backroad in Texas or in a huge urban high school on a bustling avenue in Manhattan. The scores, on a scale of 1 for the lowest and 5 for the highest, are submitted to the institutions of higher education that the students plan to attend, and it is up to each college to decide how much consideration to give the work.

Advanced Placement was one more powerful lever for dislodging the boulders that for so long obstructed the path between high school and college. It creates a middle ground for dealing with the concerns of those who proclaim that, regardless of intellectual capacity, youngsters should remain with their peers as long as they are of high school age. Even if institutions of higher education give no recognition whatsoever to the work, it is still a way of bolstering the high school curriculum. Harlan P. Hansen, director of Advanced Placement for the College Board since 1956, talks of the "strength and sparkle" that the program adds to high schools. "AP teachers and their departments find all their courses enriched through what the program has encouraged them to do," he said.[4]

Advanced Placement has inspired the creation of a host of similar programs on a smaller scale. Whatever the label, though, the goal is the same: accelerating the educational process to allow students of high school age to take college-level work. Generations ago, when colleges were little more than high schools, there was less need for this approach. The best achievers merely left the confines of grammar school and entered what was essentially a high school/college. But as high schools became formal entities and carved out their place in the educational hierarchy during the late nineteenth century, the boundaries between the two sectors were more clearly delineated, a development that was a mixed blessing.

A major step in this direction was the formation of the Committee of

17

Ten by the National Education Association in 1892. The august panel, headed by Charles W. Eliot, the Harvard president, produced a report the following year prescribing a four-year high school curriculum that has influenced the structure of high school education until this day. There was suddenly a Holy Writ, endorsed by the elite, for dividing the waters which were under the firmament from the waters which were above the firmament.

Shortly after the turn of the century the scope of a high school education was further delineated in terms of the requisite courses needed to complete a college preparatory program. This became known as the Carnegie unit system because The Carnegie Foundation for the Advancement of Teaching was the major force behind this effort.

Finally, in 1918, the territory of the high school was marked off with unmistakable boundaries by yet another report, *The Cardinal Principles of Secondary Education*, from a committee sponsored by the National Education Association. And so it was that high schools and colleges staked out the provinces of their courses.

Formalizing any structure seems to create a need to protect turf. Once high schools got hold of students who were clearly their own, they quickly grew reluctant to share those youngsters with colleges. On the other hand, colleges sought to reinforce their own niche in the hierarchy, becoming ever more careful about whom they accepted, wanting to demonstrate to the world that only those with the proper prerequisites could gain entrance. What better way to promote exclusivity than to keep certain people out of the hallowed halls of higher learning!

Acceleration is the giant step that carries a student well beyond the work usually assigned to one of his age. It happens when the needs of students are placed above the claims that schools and colleges have on students. After the twelve colleges and universities in the Early Admission Program showed their willingness to confront the problem, it was easier for other institutions to do the same.

There are always ways to achieve such breakthroughs when schools and colleges have the desire. It was interesting in the spring of 1982, as the funding for Social Security survivors benefits was expiring, to see how many colleges and universities found it possible to accept students who had not completed high school in order to make them eligible for aid under the program. The students had to have full time college status by May 1 to qualify. Somehow, the high schools found methods for letting students maintain a dual enrollment status so they could be eligible for their diplomas.

Some institutions, including the University of California at Berkeley, have had longstanding programs for bringing high school students onto their campuses. At Berkeley, the Accelerated High School Student Program is aimed at seniors in the Bay Area who have demonstrated their potential for doing college-level work. Their high school principals must nominate them for the program, and parents have to give their consent.

The students must continue to spend at least four periods a day at their high schools, where they remain officially enrolled. They are restricted to no more than two courses per quarter at Berkeley and may earn up to a maximum of 10 academic credits from the university as accelerated students.

High school students in the accelerated program sit in regular undergraduate courses at Berkeley and are not separated into classes of their own. They are expected to do the same work as the other university students and are graded on the same basis. If they eventually enroll in Berkeley the credits they earn count toward their degree requirements and if they enroll elsewhere they can apply to have the credits transferred. The list of courses at Berkeley in which high school students have participated reads like an undergraduate transcript, cutting across subjects from anthropology to geology to Italian to physics and sociology.

Where there is the will, there is surely a way. In fact, there is already more happening around the country than many observers realize in order to permit high school students to accelerate their work. The Carnegie Council on Policy Studies in Higher Education, in a review of college catalogues in 1976, discovered that high school students had access to courses at about 40 percent of the two-year community colleges and 16 percent of four-year liberal arts colleges. This comes on top of advanced placement and other opportunities for college-level work in the high school itself.

Yet, in most places, much of what happens by way of cooperation is crude and not as carefully planned as at Berkeley. Sometimes it is merely a student here or there acting on his own to enroll at a nearby college

19

for a course in the evening. Many high schools have made no effort whatsoever to coordinate their class schedules and academic calendars with neighboring colleges.

From a purely selfish point, high schools have every reason to want to be especially adamant about holding onto their students during the 1980s. A drop in the birthrate during the late 1960s and early 1970s means that high school enrollments are falling now in most school districts. The size of the nation's high school graduating class—3.1 million in 1979—will decline by 26 percent by 1991, according to figures compiled by the Western Interstate Commission on Higher Education.[5] In the Northeast and the Middle West the trend is being exacerbated by emigration to the Sunbelt.

Academic acceleration that involves high school students taking some or all of their courses on college campuses threatens to erode enrollments in high schools, where funding is usually based on the number of students. Meanwhile, the colleges and universities themselves face the prospect of declining enrollment during the remainder of the decade and have much to gain through programs that bring students to campuses at earlier ages. Thus, for the next several years efforts at acceleration may be tangled in a web of self-interest.

Therefore, programs like Syracuse University's Project Advance will be especially attractive to high schools. Project Advance permits students to earn college credits without leaving their high school classrooms, thus keeping enrollments intact and posing no financial threat to the school systems. Youngsters who successfully complete a Project Advance course are guaranteed credits from Syracuse and are considered as entitled to a transcript as a student who has studied on the campus. If the student decides to attend Syracuse, the credits are waiting there to be claimed. If he attends some other institution, a transcript will be sent by Syracuse.

Seventy-five high schools in four states—New York, New Jersey, Massachusetts, and Michigan—are participating in the program. In six different subjects, ranging from biology to sociology, the program uses the same material and the same tests given to freshmen in the introductory courses on the Syracuse campus. Research comparing the performance of students who take the courses in high schools with those who take them at the university shows very similar achievement.

The high school itself decides which students to admit to the courses. Syracuse requires only that the student has completed the normal curriculum through the eleventh grade. This means, for example, that the student has already taken a high school course in biology or chemistry and that the Project Advance course comes on top, and not as a substitute for, the high school course. Thus, almost all of the participants are high school seniors, usually getting both high school and college credit for the courses.

While aimed at students, Project Advance also is a program with benefits for teachers. The high school teachers selected to teach these college-level courses have credentials, according to Syracuse officials, that would qualify them to teach the same course on a college campus. They almost always have graduate degrees and at least five years of teaching experience in the subject area. Franklin P. Wilbur, director of Project Advance, finds it ironic that some observers challenge the credentials of the teachers, and, in effect, the credibility of the course.

"At least some bias exists in the credential challenge," he stated, "especially given that many high school teachers are better qualified to teach introductory college courses than are some of the college teachers to whom the job is usually delegated. Graduate teaching assistants or new Ph.D.'s (who often teach these courses) may have little or no teaching experience and minimal interest in teaching a freshman course; yet, because they are college teachers, their credentials are not challenged as readily as those of high school teachers."[6]

Project Advance helps high school teachers feel better about what they are doing. It also gives them a source of regular exposure to colleagues in higher education. Every Project Advance class is visited at least once a semester by a representative from Syracuse. Also once a semester, Syracuse faculty members meet as a group with the high school teachers from the same disciplinary area. This all comes on top of intensive summer workshops of 7 to 10 days in which Syracuse professors discuss common problems with high school counterparts who are teaching the same courses.

According to the university, Project Advance is not a moneymaker. It takes in just enough to cover expenses. Nor does it draw very many more students to the university than would be likely to attend in any event. So why does Syracuse bother with Project Advance?

"The opportunity to influence directly the quality of instruction (in English composition, for example) for high school seniors, some of whom will arrive on campus the following year, is an opportunity that many college professors interested in curriculum development eagerly accept," said Wilbur. "Moreover, if the program is a success and the students and their parents associate the sponsoring college or university with an improvement in high school programming, the college or university may attract new or better students (even though it may be making the effort to ensure wide portability of the education credit earned through the program to other institutions)."[7]

Operating on a more limited scale, Kenyon College in Ohio has its School/College Articulation Program through which six private schools are able to offer courses that lead to college credits. Kenyon, like Syracuse, awards its credits to students who successfully complete the courses in their high schools and a Kenyon transcript is sent to whichever college the student decides to attend.

Kenyon's involvement in such an effort is one of history's little triumphs. It was the late Gordon Chalmers, president of Kenyon three decades ago, who was a moving force in the creation of the Advanced Placement program. The steering committee for the School/College Articulation Program is made up of representatives of Kenyon and the six participating private schools. A recent attempt to extend the program to a nearby public high school failed after an insufficient number of students registered for the course that was to be offered.

Not all of the recent efforts to enrich the high school curriculum have been tied to institutions of higher education. High schools can undertake enrichment on their own. An excellent example is the International Baccalaureate program. Using a prescribed curriculum during the junior and senior years, participating schools offer students courses that, when taken in the entire two-year package, are recognized by some colleges and universities for as much as a year of academic credit.

There are 177 secondary schools in 43 countries that participate in the program, and 67 of these schools—some private, some public—are in the United States and Canada. One of these is the new Armand Hammer United World College of the American West, a secondary school on the grounds of a former resort in Montezuma, New Mexico. It is a private boarding school that has built its curriculum around the International Baccalaureate. Teen-agers from several dozen countries pursue their high school education at the school.

Wherever it is offered, the International Baccalaureate consists of three courses that are studied for two years each, and three that are studied for one year each. For students in the United States, this means the study of English, a foreign or classical language, a social science, a natural science, mathematics, and a sixth subject selected from among art, music, computer science, or an extra course in one of the required areas. A seventh course, "Theory of Knowledge," is mandatory for the two years, braiding the strands of the other courses into a unified intellectual experience.

Examinations for all of the courses are prepared and graded at the IB headquarters in Geneva. It is possible to prepare students for these examinations in courses in regular high schools that include students who are not pursuing the International Baccalaureate. The teachers, however, must add the depth and breadth for the students in the class who are pursuing the IB.

A number of colleges and universities around the world have agreed to admit automatically any student who is a product of the International Baccalaureate program. But officials of the program have had difficulty getting institutions of higher education in the United States to recognize the IB. Thus, for most American participants, IB provides enrichment but, unlike advanced placement, leads to no academic credits.

Among the most extraordinary efforts to reach out to youngsters on the precollegiate level has been that of Johns Hopkins University in behalf of the gifted. It is not so much a cooperative venture between a university and the high schools as it is between a university and the students themselves. Julian C. Stanley, a psychology professor at Hopkins, laid the foundation for the program in 1971, when he sought a way to identify young mathematical geniuses. He wanted to create a program for allowing them to work closer to their capacities than the traditional secondary school curriculum permitted.

Soon, there was the Study of Mathematically Precocious Youth, which was built around an annual search for students gifted in mathematics. The program focuses on youngsters in the seventh grade and uses the

Scholastic Aptitude Test in mathematics to identify the most able of them. Scores in the 700's—the same scores that help get high school seniors into the nation's most selective colleges—set these unusual students apart from their 13-year-old peers. Hopkins has extended the search in a quest for other expressions of brilliance and now has a program for the Verbally Gifted Youth, following similar identification procedures and using the verbal SAT.

Once they are identified, the youngsters are encouraged to choose from several different approaches designed to help them. Integral to all is a desire to let the students soar through the curriculum as quickly as they are able—even if that means, as it frequently does, pursuing college-level work while still of high school age.

Courses on the university campus itself are thrown open to the students, and more than a few have raced through the secondary curriculum, or in rare instances, skipped it altogether, and entered the university at the age of 15 or 16 or younger. "I didn't feel at all out of place in skipping four grades and going to college," said a student who went on from Hopkins to become a doctoral candidate in computer science at Cornell by the time he was 20 years old.[8]

Students who remain enrolled in their junior high schools or senior high schools, as most do, have the opportunity to participate in a Saturday program at Hopkins throughout the regular academic year, as well as at satellite centers that have been established in other states. Some youngsters and their parents travel two or three hours each way for the Saturday program. "After a quick breakfast last Saturday, I took off with my mother in the family's station wagon and learned more in two hours than I had all week at school," one student said.[9]

In a German course comparable to that given freshmen at Hopkins, the young students in the Saturday class completed the textbook two months earlier than the college students. All of those in a Writing Skills course outscored the average college freshman on the College Level Examination Program in English Composition. Seven of the 12 students in the classics course received A's from instructors who administered the same tests and applied criteria identical to those used with the university's freshmen.

There are also summer institutes for gifted junior and senior high school

24

students. The sites in 1982 were the campuses of two colleges in Pennsylvania—Dickinson and Franklin and Marshall. Courses were given in such areas as Latin, computer science, biology, psychology, composition, German, astronomy and chemistry. Students, on the average, completed two high school mathematics courses in three weeks of instruction during the summer program, according to officials. Furthermore, a quarter of the participants completed all four and a half years of their high school precalculus mathematics education in the three-week period.

In their own schools, the students are encouraged to take courses up to their ability even if this means that an eighth grader goes to a nearby high school to sit with seniors in a calculus class. They are also advised to earn as much advanced placement credit as they can. Depending on the individual, various enrollment patterns are possible, combining classroom experiences in junior high school, high school, and college. The Center for the Advancement of Academically Talented Youth at Hopkins coordinates the programs and provides counseling to both students and their parents.

The Hopkins model has been picked up by several institutions, including Duke, Northwestern, and Arizona State, so that 13-year-olds in other regions of the country are also getting the chance to move through the curriculum at a speed more appropriate to their ability.

In the days ahead, colleges and universities should work together to overcome the tyranny of time. Increasingly, students should be free to move at their own pace to make more flexible the transition from school to college.

25

CHAPTER IV

Preparing Teachers

IT IS A SAD COMMENTARY on American education that a book about *partnerships* can say very little about teacher preparation, which is, or should be, the most important connection between the nation's colleges and schools. The whole relationship between schools and colleges pivots on this essential function. Yet, historically, the preparation of teachers has been dominated by higher education. The schools have had little to say about it and are rarely consulted.

The result is endless finger-pointing about the quality of teaching in the schools. The schools are criticized for not providing adequate incentives to attract the most able high school graduates into the classroom. Colleges, on the other hand, are criticized for admitting poor students into schools of education and for teaching too much theory. Everyone seems to agree that the quality of teaching is the key to the quality of education. But there is little agreement about how teachers should be selected and prepared for their work. Ironically, there also is little effort to involve the schools in the one function of higher education—training teachers—that, in the end, affects them most profoundly.

Although the lack of collaboration in this matter is to be regretted, some colleges are making promising efforts to improve the selection of students to be trained to teach.

Beginning in the fall of 1982, students seeking admission to the teacher training programs at Pennsylvania State University and seven other institutions of higher education around the country had to pass a battery of tests. The eight institutions decided it was time to be more selective in choosing their students, and they settled on the same way of doing it. "We're hoping to increase the quality of the candidates going into teaching," said Edward R. Fagan, an education professor at Penn State.[1] He is directing the efforts of the consortium, which, in addition to his own institution, is made up of the University of South Dakota, the University of Pittsburgh, the University of Cincinnati, the University of Georgia, California State College at Bakersfield, the University of Tennessee, and the University of Wisconsin.

The consortium is trying to weed out the least qualified teaching candidates. Four examinations make up the battery. There are a reading test and a writing test—including an actual writing sample—that have been adapted from examinations produced by the Educational Testing Service. There is a five-minute test of speaking skills, recorded on a tape, that is being used for the first time in the country. The fourth test examines a student's ability to recognize inferences and make critical evaluations.

All eight institutions will use the same cutoff points on the tests as a basis for admissions to their teacher training programs, and, at Georgia, passing the tests will be a criterion for getting into the university. In most cases, students apply to enter the teacher training programs at the end of the sophomore year. Some students who do not pass the tests are to be admitted provisionally, and will have to take remedial work. But if they fail to pass the tests after remediation they are to be counseled out of teacher training.

The connection between the quality of teacher preparation and the quality of precollegiate education is the most obvious link in the chain that connects the two sectors. The level of instruction can be no better than the people to whom it is entrusted. Yet, for years, virtually any college student who wanted to become a teacher was accepted into a teacher training program. This lack of selectivity was not an issue as long as confidence in the public schools remained strong.

It was only when the indicators by which the public schools are judged turned negative that the nation grew concerned that perhaps teaching was no longer drawing capable men and women to its ranks. The extent of the problem is reflected in surveys conducted in connection with both the Scholastic Aptitude Test and the American College Testing Program. In each case, the high school seniors indicating that teaching is their prospective college major are among those getting the very lowest scores. All across the country, decision makers have started reconsidering the

28

requirements for entering teacher training and for getting into the profession after winning a degree.

"We test lawyers. We test CPA's. We test any number of professionals and they're not insulted. Why shouldn't we test people who are going to be responsible for the education of our children?" asked Harold Wiser, chief of teacher education for the Pennsylvania Department of Education.[2]

Yet, the harsh fact is that the effort to raise standards for entrance into the teaching profession comes when the public schools are almost in a position of having to accept whomever they can get. The prejudice and social mores that pushed legions of outstanding young women into teaching in prior generations have changed. Fortunately, women are no longer blocked from entering a host of fields that were formerly open only to men. The difficulty for the teaching profession is that women are now encouraged to become physicians, engineers, and banking executives, and, like men, they are not likely to settle for the low salaries and unappealing working conditions in the classroom.

Tests may make it harder for poor students to get into teaching, but where are schools of education going to find the candidates to pass those tests? The passing point on the tests may have to be set low simply to get enough candidates. Raising entrance requirements is a fine idea, but it must be coupled with efforts to attract more good candidates for the teaching profession.

If the best students are not knocking on the doors of schools and colleges of education, then these institutions ought to go out and get them. If the ablest students are deciding as undergraduates to major in mathematics, science, and the liberal arts, then they are the ones who should be induced to accept jobs in the public schools. The work to be done in the nation's classrooms is too important to leave to the mediocre.

Changing the situation is not easy when young people who have majored in mathematics, for example, can enter the computer field at higher salaries than they would earn after a career as teachers. Nor is it easy to sell young people on the virtues of teaching in the schools when the corridors of some big city high schools are as dangerous as the streets in frontier-era Dodge City.

Some would call it impractical to expect able students to enter teaching.

29

Yet, idealism is being wed to practicality at such places as the University of North Carolina at Chapel Hill, where a fresh attempt has been launched to lure better qualified candidates to elementary and secondary school teaching. A not so new idea, the Master of Arts in Teaching, is the vehicle for this effort. The MAT flourished in the early 1960s, when John F. Kennedy awakened a generation to the virtues of public service. Young liberal arts majors marched with zeal into MAT programs that would equip them with the credentials to carry their revolution into inner city classrooms. A more pragmatic impetus was added to the MAT in the late 1960s, as some liberal arts graduates saw the MAT as a writ of safe passage into temporary work that would keep them far from the dangers of Vietnam.

The attraction of the MAT faded during the late 1970s. Not only had the military draft ended, but it was a period during which the siren called careerism lured liberal arts majors to professional schools and the abundant riches they imagined awaiting them in medicine, law, dentistry, and business. Chapel Hill has dusted off the MAT and infused it with renewed substance. The graduate school administers the program under the supervision of a committee of faculty members that includes professors from the College of Arts and Sciences and the School of Education.

Almost all of the 23 students chosen to initiate the program in 1982 had majored as undergraduates in the biological or physical sciences, mathematics, or English. They have agreed to become secondary school teachers in these subjects. Funds from the Lyndhurst Foundation in Chattanooga have made each of the students a Lyndhurst Fellow, carrying a stipend of $6,000 plus a waiver of tuition and fees for two semesters and for up to two summer sessions. Once they get their master's degrees, the new teachers must work for at least three years in the schools of North Carolina or Tennessee, preferably in the rural areas of the states.

The students pursue their graduate education primarily in the subject of their undergraduate major, taking at least 18 hours of courses in their disciplines. A minimum of six hours is required in the School of Education to meet teacher certification regulations. Each student is guided by a team of mentors—a faculty member from the School of Education and a faculty member from the disciplinary department.

"Most likely, I could have made more money if I had gone into industry, but I think teaching is a valuable way of affecting our society in a positive direction," said Lyndhurst Fellow Vickie Mayer Bassett, a biology major with a degree from Cornell. "My special interest is in human biology and I hope to be able to take ideas and present them to students on a level they will be able to appreciate and use."[3]

Another Fellow, Julie Graves, was a mathematics major at Oberlin and has been a mathematics editor for a textbook publisher. She also taught in the Peace Corps in Fiji and has volunteered as a tutor in schools. She likes the idea of being able to follow her interest in mathematics through graduate study without having to get weighted down by educational methods courses. "Something like the Lyndhurst Fellowship encourages people with good mathematics backgrounds to teach in the public schools instead of going to work at a place like Xerox," Graves said. "If teachers who aren't very good in math are the ones teaching it then students won't like math and won't consider teaching it when they are adults. So, each generation gets math teachers who are progressively more uninspiring."[4]

Underpinning the Lyndhurst Program is a feeling that some able people have been dissuaded from entering teacher preparation programs by a belief that too many education courses were required and that quality teachers were not appreciated by local school systems. Perhaps what is happening at Chapel Hill is a sign that colleges and universities can counteract these views and do more to induce abler students to consider teaching careers in elementary and secondary schools. The program encourages the graduates to remain in teaching by providing them with a short refresher course after their third year as teachers, an approach used by the Danforth Foundation to help keep young scholars in college teaching.

All of this is in keeping with an obligation to elementary and secondary education that the University of North Carolina at Chapel Hill and other colleges and universities are increasingly recognizing. "As we watch the public schools decline," said Christopher C. Fordham III, chancellor of the Chapel Hill campus, "the universities are really part of the problem because we educate the teachers."[5]

The connection between higher education and precollegiate education is especially palpable when a teacher training institution has a laboratory school. Handled properly, it can be the fillip that propels professors out of the ivory tower and into the sort of hands-on experiences that make a difference in education. All laboratory schools, however, have not been the centers of research and development that their sponsors would like to believe. Sometimes such institutions have been little more than low-cost preparatory schools for the precocious children of faculty members and the relationship with the sponsoring college has produced little interaction between professors and teachers.

Nevertheless, at their best, laboratory schools have been places where models of elementary or secondary education could be implemented, places where those who work in higher education have been able to join forces with their colleagues at the precollegiate level to perfect the process of schooling. For years, laboratory schools were the principal link between the two levels of education as far as any sort of cooperative ventures were concerned. Thus, it was a blow to this relationship as the number of laboratory schools shrank during the 1970s. Jerry Duea of the University of Northern Iowa estimates that only about 95 laboratory schools remain in the country and that financial pressures were the main reason for this decline, which may well continue.[6]

Raising teacher-training standards is overdue. And yet, once again the moves are all too often unilateral, not collaborative. Colleges decide who will be admitted to the program and what the program should be with little or no consultation with the school.

What we need, perhaps, is not a rebirth of the campus ''lab'' school, which all too often become the place for children of professors. Rather, what is needed are laboratories in the communities' schools where classroom teachers are more fully involved in apprenticeship programs, working closely with prospective teachers.

The continuing education of teachers is, of course, another matter. Here examples of cooperation are more numerous.

Summer courses for teachers are not unusual, but at Chapel Hill select science and mathematics teachers who studied on the campus during the summer had weekly meetings throughout the year. Called the Middle School Math and Science Program, it involved teachers from the sixth through the ninth grades, who then came back for a second summer to tie it all together. Tuition was free for the participants and the credits they received could be applied toward graduate degrees.

Institutions of higher education are especially well positioned to design programs that relieve classroom teachers' feelings of isolation. Teachers of the same subject in a number of small school systems, for instance, can be pulled together by a college or university to join ongoing programs that link them with colleagues whose concerns are the same as theirs. Imagine what a college in a rural region could do for all of the science teachers in the surrounding school systems if it brought them together on a regular basis, not only to meet with each other, but to discuss their field with the college's own science faculty.

All the talk about higher standards for new teachers, even if translated into action, would have a limited immediate effect on what happens in classrooms. What will make the biggest difference in improving the schools will be bolstering the skills and morale of those who are already on the job. They form the largest portion of the group that will be teaching in the schools during the 1980s. So colleges and universities must plan to work with those they trained in previous years in order to bring about profound improvements in elementary and secondary education. This requires more than worn-out approaches to in-service education. All too often, in-service courses have done little more than generate income for institutions of higher education while providing teachers with empty academic credits that some of the teachers sought merely to boost themselves up the salary steps to higher pay.

What will be needed are more programs that embody the attitudes that led to the New England Studies Institute at Dartmouth. This interdisciplinary program has examined regional issues from a historical and cultural context. The concept originated with a high school teacher, who wrote the funding proposal to the National Endowment for the Humanities. Professors from Dartmouth's departments of art, history, and English and its Resource Policy Center work with more than two dozen elementary and secondary teachers each summer.

"Any gulf that might exist between an Ivy League institution and a remote union high school in the Northeast Kingdom is bridged by a cooperative model which has included a first-hand secondary school perspective in every step of the institute's design and implementation," said Alan Fraker, coordinator of the program at Dartmouth and a member of the faculty at Deerfield Academy. "The result, I believe, is a program fine-tuned to the teacher and a faculty who can truly work with, rather than lecture to, high school educators."[7]

Clearly, higher education has abundant resources in the humanities to share with elementary and secondary schools. The range of specialties in history, literature or philosophy, not simply at Dartmouth, but at any medium-sized institution of higher education far exceeds anything that even the largest high school possesses. The schools should be able to borrow some of this expertise. While few high schools can afford to maintain on their faculties someone who teaches courses exclusively on American history, there are universities with many such people, and they can enrich the quality of high school instruction. A professor, for instance, should confer with the history, literature, art, and music teachers of a particular high school and help them develop interdisciplinary units that offer cultural dimensions of American history seldom available to high school students.

Furthermore, for the millions of high school graduates who will not enter degree-granting programs, the experience could provide what might well be their last formal exposure to the humanities. If there is to be a foundation built for a lifetime of enjoyment of literature and the arts for such people, then the mortar will have to be applied at this time. The Commission on the Humanities identified the involvement of colleges and universities as an essential factor in any attempt to upgrade the humanities at the lower school level. "Because schools change slowly, we endorse models of school-college collaboration that emphasize long-term cooperation," stated the commission's report.[8]

One organization puts schools in contact with humanists for just such purposes. The National Humanities Faculty, founded in 1968, is a group of some 700 people who teach at colleges and universities throughout the country. They have agreed to make themselves available to meet with school teachers to help them strengthen their grasp of the humanities, improve the quality of their teaching in the humanities, and assist them in course and curriculum development.

The National Humanities Faculty has no preconceived packages of materials or programs to give to the schools. The professors who visit the schools respond to needs as described by the teachers and administrators.

34

Schools submit ideas for projects and the staff of the National Humanities Faculty chooses the ones in which it wants to participate. Once selected, a project is assigned a National Humanities Faculty representative who visits the schools as an adviser, meeting several times with a core group of teachers and administrators from the school. One member of the core group becomes the academic coordinator of the project and either the principal or assistant principal of the school becomes the project administrator. The National Humanities Faculty recognized early that without a firm commitment from the school's administration, projects were in jeopardy.

Once these mechanisms are in place, the adviser from the National Humanities Faculty arranges for other professors with the kind of expertise the school needs to visit and help the teachers develop their project.

The project belongs to the school, not to the National Humanities Faculty, which serves basically as a consulting firm. During the summer following the school year in which this planning is done, five or six people from the core group join those from core groups of other schools around the country in workshops lasting several weeks. They have a chance to refine their ideas and to hone their grounding in the humanities. Finally, back at school, they implement the project. The entire cycle lasts eighteen months.

Projects in which the National Humanities Faculty is involved are as varied as the humanities themselves. There has been a program to teach grammar and writing at a school in the mountains of West Virginia by using the region's folklore, music, and history. Another program in a typical small industrial town in Indiana led to teaching literature and history by having students interview their parents and grandparents about the impact of the Depression and then supplement the interview with appropriate readings.

Benjamin DeMott, Andrew W. Mellon professor of the humanities at Amherst College, is among the better known members of the National Humanities Faculty. He has found the experience very similar to being a member of a curriculum committee at his own college—full of the same politics and intrigue. In other words, faculty life in a junior high school or a high school is not necessarily any freer of personality clashes than in higher education. What this means, DeMott has discovered, is that professors who agree to help their precollegiate colleagues should not approach the task with naiveté.

"Once you are there," DeMott observes, "you may say you are just a visitor, but you are into it up to your ears and you are seen as an ally of the teacher who arranged to bring you to the school. You have to figure out how to enlarge the team and start building bridges immediately. Once they trust you, you are treated with warmth and you get a sense of common enterprise. When you do something like this, you get to know more about where your students come from."[9]

As anyone in education knows, however, these are not boom times for the humanities. The federal government's National Endowment for the Humanities is still the main benefactor of the National Humanities Faculty, but its annual contribution has dropped and the program is now operating on an annual budget of about $500,000, which includes donations from several major foundations. The humanists who visit the schools generally receive a daily stipend of $150, scarcely the kind of sum that inspires them to participate for the financial rewards. The organization, after making its headquarters for several years near historic Concord, Mass., has relocated to the campus of Emory University, outside of Atlanta. It is trying to prepare for a future in which the National Humanities Faculty will be able to rely more on foundations and corporate sources for a larger proportion of its budget.

In the past, professors representing the National Humanities Faculty have often been assigned to work with schools far from their own colleges and universities. Under the prodding of the National Endowment for the Humanities, the National Humanities Faculty is making certain some of its projects involve groups of schools and colleges in the same geographic area. The model of the Yale-New Haven Teachers Institute helped inspire this approach. "If every middle-sized city with a strong university could throw the resources of that university into its school system the way Yale is doing in New Haven, it would be quite a boost," said Richard H. Ekman, director of the Division of Education Programs of the National Endowment.

What Yale is doing, specifically, is helping its local school system with curriculum and staff development. The Yale-New Haven Teachers Institute, begun in 1978, bridges the usual barriers between town and gown with a program that enables about 80 teachers a year from the city's secondary schools to study with senior professors on the campus of the ivy league university.

The teachers participate in seminars that start each March and run through July, the topics determined by a panel of teachers from the school system. The purpose is not only to enlarge their theoretical knowledge, but also to allow the teachers to prepare curriculum units that they can take back to their schools and use the following year. Each curriculum unit is a minimum of 15 typewritten pages in length and contains objectives, strategies, suggested classroom activities, and bibliography lists for both teachers and students.

"Ongoing curriculum development is important and the Institute is a way of doing this," said Ben Gorman, a teacher at Fair Haven Middle School in New Haven. "People in New Haven have always had some access to Yale, but there was nothing like this in which professors and teachers worked so closely together in ways that have an impact on the public school students."[10]

Furthermore, program participants, who are called "fellows," have the opportunity to become members of the university community. They are listed in the Yale directory and enjoy privileges in the libraries and other facilities. This, of course, is no small matter for public school teachers, so many of whom around the country have been conditioned to a professional life in which the amenities are so few that a free cup of coffee is a valued perquisite. For their participation in the program, the teachers are paid a $650 stipend.

A poll of the New Haven teachers who have been fellows at Yale through the Institute revealed that, for almost half of them, the chance to participate in the program has been an important factor in deciding to remain as a public school teacher in New Haven.

The money to make this possible has, until now, come mainly from the National Endowment for the Humanities. There has also been a commitment of funds from 50 businesses in New Haven, a notable and unusual contribution undoubtedly reflecting a realization that improving the level of instruction in the public schools will be a boon to the entire community. Most recently, the NEH announced a three-year grant of

$368,516 to the program. In addition, Yale has set out to raise a $4 million endowment to make the program permanent. This will supplement annual operating funds provided by the city and the university.

The range of offerings in the spring of 1982 was typical of the Institute. Seven separate seminars were running—"Society and Literature in Latin America," "Autobiography," "The Constitution in American History and American Life," "Society and the Detective Novel," "An Unstable World: The West in Decline?" "The Changing American Family," and "Human Fetal Development."

Each of the participants in any one seminar would use the material to serve his or her own special needs, shaping it into a custom-made curriculum and, in a way that guaranteed each would come up with something different from the same seminar. Toward the end, each participant prepared an individual reading list in consultation with the professor. The process of writing and rewriting the curriculum unit under the direction of the professor is one of the most important features of the program. All of the units are published in a book that is then made available to teachers throughout New Haven.

Linda Powell's experience illustrates how this works. A recent seminar in which she participated was devoted to a study of British colonialism, and Powell used it to write a three-week curriculum unit on modern China. "I was able to talk about China in connection with what it did to stand up to colonialism," she said. "This program is a way to study what you know you are going to need to teach; you don't have to worry about a prescribed set of readings you may never use."[11]

Another outgrowth of the program, which is directed by James R. Vivian, has to do with the relationships that are nurtured between New Haven teachers and members of the Yale faculty. "Most of the people I taught a year ago are still in touch with me," said Robin W. Winks, a Yale history professor. "There is a growing willingness on the part of the New Haven teachers to see the university as a resource. A teacher looking for a book on a particular subject may call and ask whether I can suggest some titles. At Yale, with a faculty that is often writing books, we can tell the teachers what books just came out and what books will soon be published.

"Most schoolteachers don't have the time to keep up with the review media," Winks continued. "The gap between the teachers and the professors is not based on talent or intelligence, but on the fact that those who teach history in high school have heavier teaching loads and less time to keep up with changing trends in the discipline. They are less likely to be in touch with the way history is taught in the university."[12]

The Yale professors often learn many things as well. Having a class full of men and women who earn their living as teachers forces professors to think about their own teaching methods. Sometimes the professors are challenged in ways that regular Yale students are unlikely to challenge them.

Furthermore, dealing with complex material that they know will eventually have to be made simpler in order to be presented to secondary school youngsters gets many of the professors to think about their subjects differently. By trying to get the teachers to shape the material for secondary school students, the professors get an appreciation of just what high school students know and do not know.

A program that began at the University of Michigan in 1978 helps the schools in a different way. In this case, unlike Yale, the university eventually enrolls a good many of the students affected by the program. It is an outreach program designed to aid high school teachers throughout Michigan—in all subjects—to train their students to be better writers.

The program is very much connected to efforts that the university has launched on its own campus to promote better writing among students once they are enrolled at Michigan. The more that the University of Michigan can do to share some of this responsibility with the state's secondary schools, the lighter the burden that the institution will eventually have to carry.

Five years ago, the faculty of the College of Literature, Science and the Arts approved new writing requirements that affected students from the time they entered the university until they were graduated. Based on an evaluation of an hour-long essay that each incoming freshman writes, the student is placed in a small tutorial class or an introductory composition class or a group exempted from lower-division writing requirements. About 80 percent of the freshmen end up in the introductory composition class. The remainder are about evenly divided between the other two groups, students so needy of special attention that they are assigned to a tutorial class or students so proficient in their writing that they are exempted from any further writing requirements until they are upperclassmen.

Something like this happens in many institutions of higher education that use placement tests. What is notably different at Michigan, however, is that all students—from those who were the least able writers to those who were the most able—must fulfill a 36-page writing requirement in one of the courses they take in their major field of study during the junior or senior year.

It does not stop there. The English Composition Board that was created to oversee the writing program on campus is the organization that carries the outreach program to the schools. It has already sent teams to 300 schools around the state, promoting a sort of consciousness-raising among the teachers.

The full-day seminars are for teachers of all subjects, not just English teachers. Having implemented a campus writing requirement in all of its majors, professors from the college have something to say about writing to high school teachers of biology, history, mathematics, and all other subjects. Representatives from the university do not actually assist the teachers in the classroom or get involved in their curriculum planning. Rather, they provide advice and moral support to the secondary teachers, encouraging their interest in good writing and helping them recognize the importance of writing to the educational process, regardless of the subject being taught.

Apparently, secondary schoolteachers are grateful for the attention. "For the first time in many schools, recruiters from the university say they are greeted warmly," said Daniel Fader, chairman of the English Composition Board. "This, they say, is because a team from the English Composition Board has preceded them into the school and has supported the teachers in their attempt to place a value on literacy. Michigan, being a world-class university, has often been suspect among high school teachers as not caring enough about high school education. The greatest value of the Board, we are told, is that it confirms and supports the university's belief in good education."[13]

The first year, a day-long conference was held for representatives of secondary schools. Other colleges and universities were also invited to send representatives. "Although a conference seemed to us to be a sensible first step, we feared that the turnout for such an event might be small," said Barbara S. Morris, associate chairman of the English Composition Board. Small indeed. Almost 600 teachers and administrators from 225 schools descended on the campus. Other conferences have followed and, even more important, the University of Michigan has sent representatives to meet with teachers and administrators in the schools.

These are typical questions that teachers ask: "How can we make students want to write more? What can we do about improving reading as well as writing ability? What can we do about the powerful, negative impact of television on the literacy of our students? How can we convince students that writing is an important skill to have in the world outside of school?"

In Bloomfield Hills, a suburban school district outside Detroit, the team from the University of Michigan shared ideas with the high school teachers, talking about techniques they were using and discussing common problems. Aaron Stander, the English coordinator in Oakland County, who helped set up this arranged marriage, was pleased by the outcome.

"A lot can be accomplished when you get college people and high school people together, but the problem to overcome is the stratification," Stander said. "University people aren't comfortable with high school people and vice versa. Sometimes a lot of it goes back to the fact that university people feel that high school people aren't particularly successful at what they do or else they would be working in universities. What impressed the teachers in Bloomfield Hills was the willingness of the University of Michigan people to come and meet with them and admit that they have problems they have to work through, too."[14]

The University of Michigan does not have all the answers. But a dialogue has been started and people are thinking about writing and talking about it. All of this led up to a three-day national conference at Ann Arbor in 1981 on "Literacy in the 1980s." The conference was sandwiched in between three days of workshops.

Michigan's program has proved so popular that its professors are now carrying the gospel of good writing into high schools in other states. Yale's program has been so helpful to the teachers of New Haven that the university is now permanently endowing it.

Such successes should come as no surprise to those who watched the growth of the Bay Area Writing Project. What began as a small program at the University of California at Berkeley expanded to cover the length and breadth of the country as the National Writing Project. At 80 sites in 33 states, schoolteachers were being brought to college campuses to learn how to be better writers so that, in turn, they could teach their fellow teachers and their students to be better writers.

The point of all this is that there is a thirst among the nation's elementary and secondary teachers for all kinds of help that will improve and ease their work. It will not be slaked by just a handful of programs by a few leading universities no matter how good those programs are. There is room for many more schools and colleges to get involved in such efforts. If the quality of the teaching in America's public schools is going to rise, then the nation's institutions of higher education can no longer afford to sit back as indifferent spectators while the schools struggle with problems that they cannot solve alone.

New school-college partnerships are required in which preservice and continuing education programs for teachers are collaboratively developed.

CHAPTER V

Blends: Experiments in Transition

As envisioned by Robert Maynard Hutchins, the last two years of high school and the first two years of college would flow together as naturally as the Monongahela and the Allegheny. This confluence of the two great streams of education was one of Hutchins' passions. "A general education, I believe, should be given between the junior year in high school and the end of the sophomore year in college," he said.[1]

And so it was that Hutchins, while president of the University of Chicago, established the College as a two-year unit having more in common with the two years that preceded it than the two years that followed. Hutchins then incorporated the last two years of the University High School into the College. Thus, education between the ages of 16 and 20 was reconstituted in a form that allowed many young people to earn the bachelor's degree at a juncture at which they might otherwise be passing from the sophomore year of college into the junior year.

In his own time, and even by today's standards, Hutchins' attitude toward the high school-college connection was radical. Indeed, it is not necessary to raze and reconstruct the framework of American education to make room for the diversity of needs, interests, and abilities that ought to be accommodated. There is a need, though, for a reorientation that allows high school and college to share some pathways, whether or not one precisely follows the route charted by Hutchins.

What is supposed to be an open thoroughfare is often an unpaved dirt road full of potholes that give discomfort to those who try to move too quickly. Courses fail to mesh in the logical sequence, and teachers at the top two levels ignore one another. The keys that open the doors at one level do not fit into the locks at the next level.

There are woefully few examples of interconnecting programs that enhance the kind of continuum that educators endorse but seldom implement. The old Pasadena Junior College as it existed in the 1920s in California is a forgotten testimony to cooperation. Like the Hutchins experiment that followed, the institution illustrated the possibilities of dealing with educational overlap. The eleventh, twelfth, thirteenth and fourteenth grades were installed under the aegis of a single institution. California even then was an outpost of the avant-garde.[2]

Sometimes, it seems that education is so wed to tradition that the rules of the marriage contract predestine stillbirth in innovation. The excessive concern with maintaining the status quo is seen in such follies as that which occurred in a small town in southeastern Ohio during the 1970s, when a young woman had to get a court order to compel a school board to let her participate in a commencement ceremony. Her crime: she had left her high school a semester early to go off to college. Authorities maintained that if she did not care enough to remain for the final part of her senior year she did not deserve to march in commencement.

It took the establishment of Simon's Rock College, which enrolled its first class in 1966, to demonstrate the meaning of Hutchins' theory for the generation of the post-Sproul protest era. Set on a 270-acre, pine-covered campus in a corner of the Berkshire Hills of Massachusetts, just over the state line from New York, Simon's Rock is a place of rugged beauty, where the majesty of New England fills the crisp autumn air at the start of each academic year. Elizabeth Blodgett Hall, the founder and chief benefactor, thought the moment had arrived for the creation of an institution that would allow restless adolescents to make constructive use of the time they might otherwise waste in high school.

Students enter Simon's Rock directly from the tenth or the eleventh grade, embarking immediately on a college-level program that awards them an associate's degree two years later. In recent years, Simon's Rock has admitted students at the end of the ninth grade as well, immersing them in a transitional program for a year before allowing them to begin college-level work.

Simon's Rock, however, is more than simply another institution that lets youngsters do college work early. It has no other mission, and that makes it profoundly different from colleges and universities with early admissions programs. Its 16-year-olds are not teen-aged flotsam in a sea of older students. The institution exists to serve only their very special needs. This means providing a support structure appropriate for a population of students who would otherwise be in high school and live at home with their parents. Guiding them in the uses of independence is a major part of the college's role.

"Late adolescence is typically a period of tumultuous change as the patterns of thinking and behavior are transformed from those of a child to those of an adult," said Eileen T. Handelman, dean of Simon's Rock and a member of its founding faculty. "A key aspect of that process is learning to make choices with the understanding that choices have consequences. Thus, both academic and social structures are designed to provide such learning opportunities with support systems to maximize the learning potential and minimize the risk of serious consequences resulting from poor judgment."[3]

Building good judgment in the youngsters at Simon's Rock has meant teaching them to recognize parameters. Faculty members are supposed to provide a kind of counseling that goes beyond simply advising the students on courses. But the faculty members are cautioned not to slip into a parental role as tempting and appropriate as that may seem. The academic program stems from this same philosophical root, offering a wide range of electives within a structure that seeks to assure a broad-based education including courses from each of the major disciplines. There is also an interdisciplinary seminar required in three of the four semesters.

Simon's Rock has had its problems. Its young students have not always been adept at reconnoitering the fuzzy boundaries that separate freedom and irresponsibility; its dedicated but overburdened faculty members have sometimes not been the mentors that the luxury of more time might have allowed. Many parents are uneasy with the idea of such an institution, and Simon's Rock might have disappeared had it not been taken over by Bard College in 1979.

Allowed to continue as a separate unit, Simon's Rock has drawn renewed vigor and sustenance from the association with Bard, and, in 1982, for the first time since its establishment, there was an enrollment of more than 300 students. The institution is also now empowered to grant the bachelor's degree as well as the associate's degree.

Simon's Rock is one response to the plaintive plea of adolescents crippled by the inertia in some high schools. While the constituency for such an institution is limited, Simon's Rock remains a paradigm from which educators can learn. The nation is always slow to embrace new configurations in education, resisting modifications that challenge the existing social structure. In retrospect, the proliferation of the community college in the post-World War II era, clashing as it did with traditional notions of what a college was supposed to be, was surely one of higher education's little miracles.

Another model of education organized around human needs rather than institutional needs is found across the country from Simon's Rock. Few schools and colleges have achieved a level of cooperation comparable to that existing between Seattle Preparatory School and Seattle University. The two institutions have pooled their resources to create Matteo Ricci College, a joint program that accepts students coming out of the eighth grade and, during the next six years, provides them with a high school diploma and a college degree.

Matteo Ricci is based largely on a curriculum of tailor-made courses, most of them interdisciplinary in scope. Much of the curriculum is mandatory, but at the college level there is room for students to pursue electives. Matteo Ricci is a lean, streamlined approach to education that avoids duplication and contains none of the gaps that sometimes leaves youngsters spinning their wheels in the senior year of high school. Part of the impetus for the establishment of Matteo Ricci in 1974 was provided by two reports from the Carnegie Commission on Higher Education: *Less Time, More Options* (1971) and *Continuity and Discontinuity* (1973).[4]

Continuity and the efficient use of time are the hallmarks of the program, which the two Jesuit institutions threw open to males and females of all faiths. The college is named in memory of the 16th century Jesuit who was instrumental in introducing Catholicism to China.

Seattle Prep's entire program is devoted to Matteo Ricci I (the high school portion of the program) so, of course, all of its teachers work full-time in the program. At the college level, though, Matteo Ricci II (the

46

college portion of the program) has only a small administrative staff and no full-time faculty members. Its professors are drawn from throughout the university, with 30 or 40 faculty members a year taking on one or two Matteo Ricci courses. They are paid through a line item transfer in the budget. One reason that the opportunity to teach a Matteo Ricci course appeals to faculty members is because the program is the university's main vehicle for interdisciplinary studies.

Matteo Ricci I includes such traditional high school courses as mathematics and foreign languages and treats the subjects in the usual manner. However, several other subjects—writing, literature, history and religion—are handled in an interdisciplinary approach through what is called a *collegio*. It is the vehicle through which these courses are taught for each of the three years. The collegio is taught by a team of teachers from the various disciplines and the instruction is organized around projects.

Science is also presented in an unorthodox manner, being organized around concepts rather than disciplines. A unit on the environment, for example, might draw from biology, physics, and geology. Another unit, or *module*, as it is called, might deal with energy. Again, the various subjects would be taught as they bear on the concept. This approach has stirred some controversy at Matteo Ricci as some educators have questioned whether it assures students of an adequate grounding in each of the disciplines. The dispute bears some similarity to that existing in graduate business education, where critics question the use of the case method as the best way to study finance, marketing, accounting, and other individual disciplines.

The interdisciplinary approach at Matteo Ricci is extended into the minor courses as well. Physical education, for instance, is more than shooting baskets; it includes the study of nutrition, recreation, and anatomy. Art includes theory, appreciation and application.

After three years at Matteo Ricci I, students move on to Seattle University for Matteo Ricci II. The interdisciplinary emphasis continues with 12 required courses making up the heart of the program. Students not in the program may also enroll in these courses. On top of this, those in Matteo Ricci II must meet the general degree requirements of the university and pursue a traditional major field of study.

A major strength of the program—its time-shortened quality—is also a major problem. Only a limited number of students are attracted to so demanding a curriculum, though it is intended for the average serious student, not for the gifted. Matteo Ricci is seen by some youngsters as a pressure cooker, and while this is good for the image of quality that officials want to project it scares off some perfectly good candidates.

Furthermore, the program depends on the carefully constructed curriculum that integrates and coordinates knowledge. Again, this is an advantage so long as a student gives Matteo Ricci six years of his or her life. It becomes a complication, though, if a young person wants to enter late or leave early.

It is a tribute to Matteo Ricci that so many institutions of higher education are willing to accept its students as full-fledged freshmen after three years of high school instead of the usual four. But this has created a new problem for the program as students begin to consider the less expensive public institutions rather than the more expensive Seattle University, a private institution.

Until now, Seattle University has depended entirely on Seattle Prep to provide the students for the upper division of the program. There is no reason, however, why the model cannot be replicated in other places and why various secondary schools around Seattle could not include Matteo Ricci programs in their curricula, with students eligible to continue onto Seattle University.

Moving away from Matteo Ricci, another response to the problem of articulation is the effort in some places to blend the last year of high school and the first year of college. This is an attempt to create a unique educational experience that is neither wholly high school nor wholly college. In some cases, students can get dual credit and lop a year off the educational process. This is the sort of setting in which the Clarkson School operates. Founded in 1977 as a division of Clarkson College of Technology in upstate New York, the school is made up of a single class, a one-year program to give young people the social and intellectual tools to build a bridge between the two levels of education.

Students in the Clarkson School live in houses near the college campus, where they spend much of their time with each other in a residential experience that is a main part of the program. As may be expected at a school under the auspices of a technical college, strong doses of mathematics and science are fed to the youngsters. But a special effort is made to give them a rounded education. A self-development Program prods them to set personal objectives in such areas of human relations and communication skills, appreciation of the arts, physical conditioning, and awareness of the place of the professional in society. It is hardly like the setting in which so many of the nation's 17-year-olds, afflicted by ennui, suffer through "senioritis" during the last year of high school.

A similar philosophy underpinned the creation of the Freshman Year Program in 1972 at the New School for Social Research in New York City. Restless students were accepted from the eleventh grade—and a few from the tenth grade—and immersed in a curriculum of college courses. The emphasis was on providing the students with the kinds of skills of inquiry and the capacity to make judgments that would enrich the next three years of college. After the year, all of the students would transfer to the institutions of their choice, usually being accepted with sophomore standing.

The Freshman Year Program continues at the New School, but it no longer has quite the significance it did. Since 1976, the New School has made it possible for students to remain enrolled and get a bachelor's degree. Fewer transfer after the freshman year and the program has lost something of the specialness that originally set it apart.

A transitional year that is a mix of high school and college could be helpful to many young people, though the opportunity for such an experience is given to few. Bridgton Academy in North Bridgton, Maine, presents a variation on the theme, having the feel of a college and the academic substance of a high school. Students attend Bridgton after being graduated from high school, but what they get is a dose of high school that they did not swallow the first time around. It is something like the postgraduate year that some students take at prep schools, but in Bridgton's case, there are no other students in the school.

Robert E. Walker, the headmaster at Bridgton, runs what is essentially a one-year preparatory school, reviewing the guts of the high school curriculum in a set of required courses. The stress is on the basic skills that youngsters will need in college. The 175 boys who attend the school are the sort who may have been too busy with social or athletic activities or simply did not care enough when they attended high school. Their records were poor and some of the students could not get admitted to any selective college, much less the one of their choice. An extra year to mature in rural Maine and additional exposure to the lessons that they tuned out the first time around, enable almost all of Bridgton's students to move into college the next year.

Many of the students attending Middle College High School in New York City had no thoughts of any college, much less a selective one. They were candidates for education's scrap heap. Kevin Johnson, for example, was a troublemaker in his junior high school, frequently brawling and suspended more than once. Johnson (not his real name) seldom did his homework and rarely turned in an assignment on time. He went to class only when he felt like going. On completing the ninth grade, his achievement scores in reading and mathematics were at least two years below grade level. Johnson had all the markings of a potential dropout.

Yet, he was prodded to enroll in Middle College High School, and the institution agreed to accept him. Despite his miserable record, it was clear in other ways that Johnson had the potential—if he could be motivated— not only to get a high school diploma, but to go to college. Middle College High School was designed for students like him. "One of our goals from the very beginning was to encourage kids to go on to higher education," said Janet Lieberman, a founder of the school and a professor of psychology at LaGuardia Community College.[5]

Middle College High School, which was created in 1974, operates under the auspices of the New York City Board of Education and LaGuardia Community College, a unit of the City University of New York. Its classes meet in one of the college's buildings, but the entire campus and all of the facilities are open to students in the high school. Situated in the predominantly industrial Long Island City section of Queens, the high school accepts students from many parts of the borough. It specifically wants youngsters like Kevin Johnson and, in fact, students from backgrounds similar to his make up most of the enrollment of the school. They are a diverse group—47 percent white, 27 percent hispanic, and 26 percent black. Girls slightly outnumber boys.

Proximity to the college is a key to the success of the high school. Though older and more settled, many of the students at LaGuardia Community College come from circumstances much like those of Johnson's.

50

The hackneyed expression of "role model" is appropriate in this setting. Most of the high school students, after a brief quieting down period, adapt themselves to fit in on the college campus. They want to be accepted. Furthermore, they quickly realize that they are in the midst of young men and women who, a few years earlier, were themselves marginal students.

LaGuardia Community College, like Middle College High School, is full of students whose ability to reach their potential was seriously in question. Half of the graduates of Middle College continue their education at LaGuardia and so students in the high school have a built-in basis for friendship with the portion of the college students who are their former classmates. Once they go on to college, they are also able to remain in contact with the high school teachers who have been a source of support to them.

Such an arrangement means that some of the high school teachers have a chance to teach in the college and the college professors have the opportunity to teach in the high school. Whenever appropriate, the high school students can take courses with the college students and use the courses to gain, simultaneously, both high school and college credits. A broad array of counseling and guidance services provided by the college are available to students at the high school, relieving the high school of much of this responsibility. The college staff helps with academic advising, psychological counseling, health services, and career guidance.

When it comes time for the high school seniors to select their colleges, they have the advantage of college counselors experienced in assisting students graduating from the community college in choosing four-year colleges in which to continue their education. The small high school of 450 students also has use of the college's gymnasium, library, laboratories, and other facilities.

Middle College has borrowed a key element from LaGuardia in imitating its internship program. Dividing the academic year into trimesters, the school has each student out for a portion of the year performing volunteer work for which credit is awarded. They help in schools, hospitals, day-care centers, and other community agencies, and by the time they are seniors many are receiving wages through their internships. At the college level, students follow the same kind of schedule, working almost entirely from the outset at paying jobs that often provide experience tied to their career goals.

The high school looks at the program as a way for youngsters to boost their egos, to feel needed. One student, for instance, who was having trouble mending his bad habits was finally turned around by the chance to be an aide in a gym class at a junior high school. Before long, he was coaching the school's basketball team and the new view he gained of himself was crucial.

"One of the great strengths of the Middle College model is that each student is assigned immediately to a career education supervisor who maintains a close relationship, both as teacher and counselor, with that student over the next three years," explained Arthur Greenberg, former principal, and Janet Lieberman. "The same faculty person serves as the student's teacher of career education courses, internship monitor, seminar leader, and career education counselor. This relationship binds together all the programmatic elements of the sequence, while at the same time, establishing the mutually trusting relationship that it is essential to maintain with troubled adolescents."[6]

The collaboration between Middle College High School and LaGuardia Community College is not perfect and has not realized its full potential. It has not led to a new curriculum that takes full advantage of the two institutions working together. Interchanges between the teachers and the professors have not been all they might be. There is still a great deal of room for teachers at the high school to develop links with their subject area colleagues in the college. What is important, however, is that the structure that may make more of this happen is now in place.

After a shaky start in the middle 1970s, the high school has a lower drop-out rate than the citywide average and its average rate of daily attendance exceeds that of the city. Eighty-five percent of its graduates go on to college. Arthur Greenberg, the former principal of Middle College, has now gone on to head another New York City high school.

"The experience at Middle College is instructive to the rest of the country in at least two ways," said Greenberg. "First, because it shows the potential of this kind of articulation when two institutions really want to make it happen. The other thing is that it shows that the level of cooperation needed to make something like this work has to be rather unusual. Even well-meaning people have difficulty making something like this work successfully. High school and college are two different cultures—different languages, a different ethos, different accrediting systems, even different calendars. Unless institutions are willing to examine themselves structurally and make accommodations, the challenge may be too great."[7]

CHAPTER VI

Minorities: A Shared Mandate

WHEN THE STATE legislature in California wanted to increase the enrollment of black and Hispanic students at the University of California in the middle 1970s, it was readily seen that whatever program was initiated would have to reach the students long before they walked onto a campus at Berkeley, Los Angeles, La Jolla, or anywhere else in the system. This lesson was learned in the grim aftermath of the assassination of the Rev. Martin Luther King, Jr., when colleges and universities across the country began displaying unaccustomed interest in recruiting minority students. Academic officials seemed to think that all they had to do was admit the students, and the future would take care of itself.

Soon, the lack of preparation among minority students was evident, and the swirl of statistics attesting to growth in minority enrollments could not obscure the equally dramatic figures showing high drop-out rates among such students. Intervention at the high school level and even sooner is necessary to get students ready for the rigors of higher education. "An engineer starts being made in kindergarten and first and second grade," said Albert Shanker, president of American Federation of Teachers.[1]

Minority students have not been well served by the educational system as it now operates. Starting at an early age, they are often set on an educational treadmill that leaves them huffing and puffing just to stay in place. Their achievement scores fall farther and farther behind as they grow older, and by the time many such students reach junior high school they are unable to do the work normally expected of children their age.

Achievement scores in reading and mathematics have faltered in big city school systems as more and more of their enrollments have become

55

predominantly minority. "In the schools, although scores are going up in some places, more black kids are being put on the dung heap every year," said Kenneth Clark, the psychologist now retired from the faculty of the City University of New York.[2] Clark, a member of the New York State Board of Regents, conducted research on the impact of racial segregation in schools that was cited by the United States Supreme Court in its landmark decision of 1954.

And so it was that the Partnership Program, started by the University of California in 1975 with state funds, focused on better early preparation as the way, eventually, to lift minority enrollments in higher education. Intervention through the program begins in the seventh grade so that minority youngsters can get sufficient information to shape their objectives in a way that will have them setting their sights on the University of California or some similar institution. Motivation is at the heart of the program. Once they reach high school, the youngsters should be enrolling in college preparatory courses and not in dead-end Mickey Mouse electives that slam the door on their future.

Five major activities characterize the Partnership Program—academic advising, role model representation, campus visits, dissemination of printed information, and meetings with parents. The eight undergraduate campuses of the University of California have taken the program into 250 junior high schools across the state. Each campus has a service area that it covers with two full-time program directors. The other campus of the university, its medical complex in San Francisco, serves the entire program with an annual summer residency at which the junior high school students spend one week being introduced to the health professions.

Students in the Partnership Program, as compared with those of similar background who are not in the program, turn out to be more likely to enroll in college preparatory courses when they reach the ninth grade. Furthermore, they get higher grades than their peers. A major accomplishment of the program has been its ability to persuade parents to cultivate aspirations for higher education in their youngsters. The failure of parents to offer such encouragement has historically hampered efforts to orient minority students toward college.

Once youngsters reach high school, the project takes on the name University Partners Program, providing services to help the students make their way through the college preparatory curriculum. Counseling and tutoring become important components of the program in high school. Much of this help is provided through the university's Academic Enrichment Program. University students or recent graduates, as well as faculty members, counsel and tutor the high school students.

The California Round Table on Educational Opportunity, in a statement last year, reemphasized the essential nature of such programs and urged an even greater commitment by schools and colleges to work together in behalf of minority students. "We are convinced that the single most effective step that can be taken toward better representation of low income and ethnic minority students in baccalaureate study, their retention once they are enrolled, and their subsequent entry into postgraduate study lies in stronger academic preparation at the junior and senior high school level for all students," the Round Table asserted.[3]

The need for early intervention of the sort involving the University of California was recognized some time ago by the Alfred P. Sloan Foundation. In 1973, the foundation initiated the Minority Engineering Program to boost the number of minority students in engineering. The emphasis was on reaching into secondary school, where students must get the prerequisite experience in science and mathematics if they are to have any hope of coping with an engineering curriculum in college.

Of the 62,839 bachelor's degrees awarded in engineering in 1981, only 4.7 percent went to blacks, Hispanics, and American Indians. These same three minority groups made up 2.5 percent of the master's degree recipients and 1.4 percent of those getting doctorates.[4] And these figures, as low as they are, represent improvements during a decade in which more attention than ever was being given to raising minority enrollments in engineering.

The Minority Engineering Program just now drawing to a close has provided $13.1 million, most of which was funneled through six regional consortia around the country. Each consortium pulled together the work of schools, colleges, industrial corporations, and community agencies to sponsor tutoring, field trips, and clubs for minority students in junior and senior high school. All of the activities were aimed at interesting youngsters in scientific careers and giving them support in the courses they would need as foundation stones for building a career in engineering.

57

An institution with extensive experience in this approach is Illinois Institute of Technology in Chicago. IIT began its program for recruiting minorities for careers in engineering in 1974 and added a similar program for careers in medicine in 1979. In each case, the efforts start by the end of the sophomore year of high school and carry through to college. It is the kind of venture no high school could embark upon alone.

"Our philosophy is based on the idea that there is a lot of talent out there and they just have to find the right young people and put the finishing touches on them,"[5] said Nate Thomas, director of the Pre-University and Minority Projects Office at IIT. The institution uses a network of former students, community people, high school teachers, and others to get leads on youngsters who might be candidates for the two programs.

During the spring of their sophomore year, the students visit the campus for a series of four workshops. They are told about the academic preparation demanded of those who want to pursue scientific and engineering careers, what subjects they will need in high school, and what it is like to be an engineer or a scientist or a physician.

In the spring of their junior year in high school, some 300 students are invited to IIT for three full-day Saturday sessions. They are organized into teams of four and compete in designing projects that test their ability to apply scientific concepts. In one case, for example, they have to build a tiny vehicle that can absorb an impact at high speed without breaking the egg that it carries as its "passenger." This is just one more step in the screening process to ferret out bright minority students for the program. Threaded through these sessions are lectures by IIT science and engineering professors.

During the summer following their junior year, the students move in separate directions during a seven-week session, with up to 150 youngsters going into each of the two programs. Those headed for engineering again form teams to compete in solving problems of design. The ones hoping for careers in medicine take mini-courses in chemistry and biology, complete with lectures and lab periods. Both groups get a generous helping of motivational activities and heaps of information about their prospective careers. Minority engineers and physicians speak to them on campus, and

58

the students visit hospitals and research sites to see how work is done. They are also tested to find academic deficiencies that need bolstering.

Much of this remedial-type work is given in classes at IIT every Saturday for 16 weeks during the students' senior year of high school. The classes are largely organized as tutoring sessions and the aim is to make certain that the students will have the academic background they will need when they walk onto a college campus the following year. College-level assignments are provided for those who are ready to tackle the work. All of the youngsters are primed to prepare them for the SAT and the ACT.

Many of the students in the engineering program concentrate on mathematics and physics during tutoring sessions that may last well into each Saturday afternoon. Those in the medical program tend to get extensive tutoring in chemistry and biology. Undergraduate assistants, some of whom are graduates of the program, help the professors in the classes. Laboratories at IIT are also made available to the students, who in some cases have had little exposure to such a setting because poor facilities were available in their high schools.

Before the senior year ends, the staff at IIT helps the students with their college applications and advises them in their search for scholarships and financial aid. Many of the students, not surprisingly, decide to attend IIT, which now graduates more minority students in engineering than any college in the country. IIT continues to be involved with the young people in the summer following graduation from high school no matter what their choice of college, giving them further counseling for college and helping them find summer jobs.

Relationships that IIT has established with a wide number of corporations have produced summer jobs for the high school graduates with such companies as Amoco, Atlantic Richfield, Cummins Engine, Eastman Kodak, and U.S. Steel. The work provides the young people with both income for college and valuable experience. In some cases, the summer jobs have been pathways to full-time employment with the companies.

For those in the medical careers program, there is a preceptorship after graduating from high school and before entering college. It usually lasts nine weeks and carries a stipend in return for working in such settings as a physician's office, a laboratory, a clinic, or some other health facility. Additional tutoring and classes are offered to the students who need it during those final months before their first year of college begins.

Wherever the students attend college, those in the medical program return for additional preceptorships during the summers before their sophomore, junior, and senior years—getting extra underpinning for their premedical training. IIT carries out this project in conjunction with a consortium of medical schools that have joined together to form the Chicago Area Health and Medical Careers Program.

Engineering students, however, do not have the benefit of such a lavish program of support once they are in college. Those who attend IIT though, are given special attention and have the advantage of the extensive ties to the school they have already built. For the students who go off to dozens of other colleges, the staff of the Pre-University and Minority Projects Office gives whatever help it can during vacations and other times that the young people may visit the campus.

What distinguishes IIT's program is its demonstration that early identification of promising youngsters can make a big difference in their lives. "It's probably the best thing that's happened to me," said Arthur Molnar, a graduate of the University of Chicago Laboratory School and a participant in the medical careers program.[6] A high school on its own might never be able to pick out all of these youngsters and even if it did, the resources would probably not be there to nurture the student's development. IIT has been able to marshal $4.2 million in government, foundation and corporate grants to make these programs work.

Engineering and medicine are professions that obviously require a great deal of early preparation. Remedial studies have been used successfully to offset deficiencies in students hoping to enter a host of nonscientific fields. But the depth of background required to embark upon an engineering or pre-medical curriculum virtually forced the recognition of the interconnectedness between what happens in high school and its implications for higher education.

Thus, it has been that medical education, one of the most selective and most demanding areas of study, is a field in which the high school/college connection has gotten the greatest attention. The numbers of minority students entering medical schools have been abysmally low, and most minority physicians are the products of black medical schools. Only 2.7 percent of medical students were blacks in 1968. There was a flush of interest in expanding the opportunities for minority members in the late 1960s and early 1970s and the Association of American Medical Colleges set a goal of boosting minority representation in the nation's medical schools to 12 percent of the overall enrollment.

Progress was swift at first, upping the black enrollment to 7.5 percent in 1975, but now the pace has slowed. Since the middle 1970s minority enrollment in medical schools has not increased.[7] This turn of events has underscored the need for better early preparation of minority students. Medical schools can be just so flexible; if schools and colleges do not act together in their efforts to provide a larger flow of qualified candidates, then even the best intentions will not produce more black and Hispanic physicians.

One organization that has recognized this is the Josiah Macy, Jr., Foundation, which is backing two model projects—one at City College of the City University of New York and the other at the University of Alabama at Tuscaloosa. Both ventures are designed to begin working with students as early as the ninth grade to prepare them eventually for success in medical school.

"Inner-city schools which educate most minority students are seriously inadequate when compared with schools graduating outstanding non-minority students," concluded a report emanating from a conference on minorities in medicine that was sponsored by three major foundations. "Few minority students from such schools reach college with sufficient preparation to undertake freshman courses in physics, chemistry and mathematics."[8]

The vehicle for the minority medical program at City College is the A. Phillip Randolph High School, created in the late 1970s as a laboratory type school run in conjunction with the college. Situated in a building on the campus, the high school, in addition to its regular enrollment, now admits 100 students a year at the ninth grade into a minischool venture known as the Macy Medical Professions Program. A recruiter visits junior high schools to find candidates for the program and to encourage them to apply. There were 1,009 applicants for the first class, 300 of whom were invited for interviews.

To help the students get off to a strong start, classes are limited to 20 students, compared with the 35 or so in the regular classes in the rest of the school. A prescribed curriculum ensures that the youngsters are exposed to the kind of academic program that ought to prepare them for premedical studies. It is a rigorous program, running longer than the regular school day, leaving almost no open spots in the schedule, and demanding at least two to three hours a night of homework. Each year, on top of the rest of the curriculum, there will be a course in critical thinking to enhance the sort of reasoning skills that are needed in all subjects, introducing the students to logic, computer use, and other tools of problem solving.

A hand-picked group of teachers has been assigned to work exclusively in the program and the courses they teach are the outgrowth of curriculum planning done by supervisors from the New York City Public Schools and faculty members at City College and Columbia. Furthermore, a tutorial program was formed using City College students. Each of the college students is assigned to tutor five high school students five hours a week.

City College, through its Sophie Davis School of Biomedical Education, is a relatively old hand at trying to improve opportunities in medicine for minority students. The biomedical program receives students directly from high school, guaranteeing them admission to medical school, and takes them through their premedical training and the first two years of medical school. It is aimed at providing primary care physicians for medically underserved areas, while improving access to medical careers for minority and low-income students. Some of the lessons learned through working with students in the biomedical program have helped shape the Macy Medical Professions Program and some staff members have been involved in both efforts.

The University of Alabama is a more recent entrant to the field. Like scientists independently striving to solve the same experiment, planners at Alabama and City College were working separately toward setting up medical careers programs for minority high school students, neither institution aware of what the other was doing. The Macy Foundation, however, learned of their activities and brought them together, finally awarding them grants at the same time, enabling one institution to concentrate on rural youngsters and the other on urban youngsters. The first group of ninth graders entered each program in 1982.

Alabama's program has been set up at five high schools in three counties. Two of the schools are in Tuscaloosa County and the other three are in neighboring Green and Hale Counties, two of the poorest counties in the United States. They also are counties in which blacks make up more than 60 percent of the population. Adults in the two counties have, on the average, completed less than nine years of formal education, low even by the standards of Alabama, one of the states with the lowest educational level.

Producing physicians who will go back and practice in the region means reaching them early, and that is exactly what the University of Alabama is trying to do for a total of 100 selected students in the five schools. The courses they take follow a carefully prescribed curriculum—just as at City College—and the planning was also done jointly by high school and university people.

Twice each semester, the high school students are brought to the Tuscaloosa campus for weekend programs in the facilities of the College of Community Health Sciences and other parts of the university. "These students are from families that traditionally have had no contact with a university, and they are at first petrified at the idea of coming on campus," said Harry J. Knopke, the project director and associate dean for academic affairs in the medical school. At the university, the youngsters are introduced to the process by which health care professionals are prepared for their fields.

A six-week summer session is scheduled to follow each academic year in order to provide tutoring and to strengthen study skills and test-taking techniques and to teach speed reading. The students will also take some regular courses during the session and work as volunteer members of health care teams in their home counties.

The program also encourages an ongoing relationship with the university by the teachers in the participating high schools. Both those directly involved with the students in the program and other teachers in school are offered in-service training during the school year and in the summer. Those who participate get adjunct appointments to the medical school faculty and the ensuing privileges. Project staff members from the university meet in person with the teachers of students in the program at least once every other week to discuss the progress of the youngsters and to deal with problems as they arise.

The very presence of the university in west central Alabama means that people in the rural, economically-deprived region have a chance for cultural and educational advantages that very likely could not otherwise be part of their lives. The university's potential contribution to the students who may end up in medical school is immeasurable, but the institution is spreading its influence in other ways as well. Part of the Biomedical Sciences Preparation Program calls for counselors to make the participating students and their parents aware of events being sponsored by the university. Students will even be encouraged, for example, to participate in the archaeological digs being carried out by the university in Moundsville State Park.

City College, on the other hand, has been doing all of its excavations above ground, ferreting out and cultivating talent in inner-city secondary schools. The Macy Medical Professions Program is a natural outgrowth of the college's expanding experience with school-aged students.

One of the earlier efforts—concluding in 1982—was the West Harlem Magnet Junior High School Project, a racially-integrated magnet school for students with demonstrated ability in science. The college was one of several city agencies involved in the venture, under which 60 youngsters visited the campus two afternoons a week throughout their junior high years for science enrichment. They studied biology at City College in the seventh grade, chemistry in the eighth grade, and earth science in the ninth grade.

Two similar projects are continuing. The Boys Harbor Senior High School Program involves 30 minority high school students who go to the campus each Saturday for extra instruction in mathematics and science. The Select Program in Science and Engineering for 480 tenth graders from 16 New York City high schools meets on the campus for 12 Saturdays each semester, providing laboratory experiences, mathematics lectures by scientists, and career counseling.

Science and mathematics teachers from the students' high schools accompany them to the college so that they can incorporate into their instruction the work that the youngsters do on the campus. Moreover, the high school teachers are counted on to sustain the spirit of the program once the students move into the final two years of high school. The program is intended to arouse the interest of the youngsters in science and to motivate them to take science courses in the eleventh and twelfth grades, hoping they become interested in science-related careers. Apparently, it is working. The first group to participate in the program has now been graduated from high school. Compared with peers who were not in the program, they were much more likely to continue in science, to get higher grades and to enroll in college, according to Harry Lustig, provost of City College and a leader in the outreach efforts.

These are just a few of the scientifically-oriented programs that City College runs for students while they are still in secondary school. There is also a Science Speakers Bureau through which faculty members who are active researchers speak with groups of high school students at their schools or on campus. Thirty of the college's scientists have enlisted in the program.

An institution need not have the distinguished scientific reputation of City College, however, to contribute to the development of minority youngsters. Several programs that the Ford Foundation has sponsored around the country since 1978 have demonstrated the possibilities for all kinds of colleges.

A notable example is SUPER in Birmingham, Ala., implemented by tiny Miles College in conjunction with the city school system. SUPER (Skills Upgrading Program for Educational Reinforcement) used retired schoolteachers to tutor school children—from the first through the eighth grade—after school hours and during the summer. Miles, a private black college, has extensive experience in dealing with underprepared students and was ideally suited to oversee such a program. Furthermore, the college draws 65 to 70 percent of its students from the Birmingham area and will probably benefit from any steps taken to wipe out learning deficits while students are still at the precollegiate level.

Nineteen retired teachers participated in the project, receiving modest pay for their efforts. They met with the students two hours a day twice a week during the school year and four hours a day, four days a week during the summer. The number of youngsters in the program usually ranged from about 200 to 300. Field trips and social gatherings were added to the program to enrich the experience for the students, almost all of whom came from impoverished backgrounds.

Although the faculty and students from Miles were not doing the tutoring, the fact that a college sponsored and organized a program for elementary school pupils was significant. Seldom does an institution of higher education take an active interest, beyond teacher training, in the education of youngsters in the early grades. But intervention cannot come too soon for deprived students and, in reaching out to first graders, Miles was taking a small step toward heading off the educational disaster that has foreclosed the future for all too many such youngsters.

CHAPTER VII

Special Models

IF SCHOOLS HAD PARENTS, Queens College would be both mother and father to the Louis Armstrong Middle School. The college has been involved in the school since its opening three years ago. Faculty members and student-teachers from the college have been integrated into the day-to-day life of the school, which runs from the fifth through the eighth grade.

This is no paper relationship. Sidney Trubewitz, an associate dean of the School of Education, spends almost all his time in the school. The agreement that cemented such firm ties was reached at the highest level between Frank J. Macchiarola, the city schools chancellor, and Saul Cohen, the president of Queens College. Both men are personally committed to the project.

The focus of this attention is a building in the East Elmhurst area of northern Queens, a potpourri of ethnicity 20 minutes by subway from Times Square. It is smack between the roar of the jets at LaGuardia Airport and the roar of the fans at Shea Stadium. The nearby Corona neighborhood, a black enclave, was the home of the musician whose memory the school honors. Carefully drawing its students from a waiting list of 1,000, the school has created a paradigm of integration reflecting the makeup of the Borough of Queens.

No teacher in the school can fail to feel the effects of the collaboration with the college. The impact can be seen in the way it impinges on just one teacher, Mary Ellen Levin, whose subject is English. Like other teachers in the school, Levin has been able to take courses free at the college. Recently, after completing one such course in computer language, she was allowed to keep her terminal and take it back to the Armstrong School to use with her students. When Levin needed a library consultant, the college sent one. The college also provided a story-telling expert to meet with her students once a week. Most semesters, Levin is assisted by a student-teacher from Queens College. She also is able to guide some of her students and their parents into the family counseling program that the college makes available for the school community.

Students and professors from Queens College are fixtures in the Armstrong School. The student-teachers are primarily responsible for the Early Bird Program permitting youngsters to arrive at school at 8 a.m., 45 minutes before the regular schedule begins, for sports and crafts activities. The college has been heavily involved in the museum that was established in the school. The guidance provided by the college has enabled the school to develop an elaborate outreach program to parents and other members of the community, an effort that includes counseling, adult education, and a host of activities that link the school to the people of Queens.

The model of cooperation developed between Queens College and the Armstrong School is not perfect, nor would it suit every pair of institutions. But it is the sort of relationship that ought to be found more frequently. Not all colleges have the opportunity to give birth to a school in the way Queens College did. All institutions of higher education can establish a special partnership with schools. It is a concept that could allow colleges and universities through the country to get involved in public education to an extent few have done.

When such projects work, one reason is probably that those representing higher education do not regard themselves as purveyors of the ultimate truth. Teachers in elementary and secondary schools are not primitives waiting for missionaries from the academic world to provide enlightenment. Rather, partnerships work because the agenda is not dictated by the colleges, but developed collaboratively with the schools.

The gulf separating those who teach in the schools from those in institutions of higher education sometimes seems too deep to overcome. The worlds of the school and the college are different at the same time that they are alike. Teachers at the two levels speak the same tongue, yet some are incapable of dialogue. One is supposed to prepare students to sit in the classrooms of the other, but neither bothers finding out what the other is doing. The curricula should mesh, but they are seldom jointly planned. It is as though workers on the Chevrolet assembly line were trying to attach wheels to a chassis on which no one had installed an axle.

"The time seems clearly right to ask college and university scholars to be less condescending in their attitude toward the schools and to ask school people to be less certain that university scholars know nothing about life in the schools," said Richard Ekman of the National Endowment for the Humanities.[1]

Actually, professors can learn a great deal about the art of teaching and a lot about students from their colleagues in the schools. Most professors have had little formal preparation for teaching. Scholarship does not automatically confer the ability to teach, and, until very recently, promotions at colleges and universities were made with little regard for one's teaching ability.

On the other hand, professors are paid, in part, to keep abreast of their fields. They have lighter teaching loads so that they will have time for scholarship. This luxury is denied those in elementary and secondary schools. They spend almost every working hour, five days a week, in front of classes, playing the role of performers who are on stage for the entire show. Ideally, members of the professoriate can be a resource to them.

One attempt to move in this direction is the work of the New York Alliance for the Public Schools. The Alliance, based at New York University, maintains a data base listing professors by areas of expertise so that they can be called on as consultants to the New York City Public Schools. When a school needs a certain kind of expert, a phone call or letter to the Alliance produces a list of up to three faculty members willing to offer assistance. Professors from the City University of New York, Fordham, St. John's, and Columbia are involved, along with those from NYU.

"I believe that we must reaffirm our commitment to a vigorous, thriving public school system," said John Brademas, the president of New York University. "Here our universities have a profound stake and special responsibility. As Ernest Boyer, president of The Carnegie Foundation for the Advancement of Teaching, has put it, 'We cannot have excellence in higher education if we do not have excellence in school.' I am pleased to say that my own institution, New York University, has been a leader in this respect. The New York Alliance for the Public Schools, organized by NYU in a joint effort with other universities in the city, is supporting a major training program to improve the leadership skills of principals in the city's 110 public high schools. A grant from the Chase Manhattan Bank has made possible this imaginative initiative."[2]

Institutions of higher education are not alone in seeking out ties with elementary and secondary education. Business and industry have also been moving in this direction. The quality of public school systems is perhaps just as important to the business community as to the higher education community. Inadequately-prepared students who cannot cope with the requirements of entry-level jobs are an employment problem, and undesirable schools are a detriment in recruiting employees whose children may have to use those schools.

"One way things are going to change is if you promote in the school system those values you represent," Frank J. Macchiarola, chancellor of the New York City Public Schools, told a gathering of executives from the Touche Ross accounting firm over breakfast one morning. "The school system requires your assistance in an institutionalized way and in a personal way."[3]

In the last three years, the New York City schools have received $973,580 from the Exxon Education Foundation, $565,000 from the Mobil Corporation and, most recently, $480,000 from Chase Manhattan Bank in conjunction with the New York Alliance for the Public Schools.

There are other ways in which business, schools, and colleges can work together. An unusual collaboration of the three sectors grew out of a $135,000 grant from Conoco Inc. in 1980 to Smith College. The college used the money to improve the teaching of writing, and, among other projects, produced a writing handbook for its students. The English chairmen at many of the high schools from which the college draws its students were told about the handbook and by 1982 Smith had sold, at cost, 40,000 of the handbooks to high schools.

In some instances, the impetus for cooperation has been the racial desegregation of schools. A good example of this is seen in Boston, where W. Arthur Garrity, Jr., a judge of the Federal District Court, built collaboration into the desegregation plan he ordered the school system to implement. Business corporations, as well as institutions of higher edu-

70

cation, were teamed up with specific schools to help try to improve the quality of education at the same time that the schools were integrating their students.

The idea of enhancing desegregation by tying it to higher quality education is so obvious that many educators apparently never thought of it. In Boston, where the resources of such prestigious institutions of higher education as Harvard and Massachusetts Institute of Technology are available, the concept is especially alluring. The participation of colleges and universities was not altogether altruistic, however, since the state provided some compensation for the cooperation.

In turn, the expertise lent by MIT, for example, helped create a new public secondary school, the Mario Umana Harbor School of Science and Technology. Faculty and staff members from MIT helped design the curriculum, train the teachers, acquire equipment, and operate the computer center. Throughout Boston during the late 1970s there were similar examples of collaboration.

From the vantage of the 1980s, though, experts feel that the venture was not all it might have been. A few institutions did as much and even more for the schools as MIT, but most did not. Furthermore, the continuing furor over desegregation and recurrent fiscal problems kept the school system in constant upheaval that militated against many good intentions.

The transition report prepared for Robert Spillane as he assumed the superintendency of the Boston Public Schools in 1981 observed that the cooperative programs with both higher education and business were impaired by a lack of a central direction and an absence of clear goals. The recommendations made at the time are relevant to all such cooperative ventures, citing the need for a single high-level coordinator, a system of evaluation, and a statement of goals and priorities for the collaboration.

There are, of course, hundreds of thousands of young people who take the diploma and run. What role can colleges and universities play in their lives? The community colleges, which have so often blazed paths that were later followed by the four-year institutions, surely can find creative forms of collaboration that will be profitable for youngsters bound for the world of work. Cooperation with schools may, in fact, be easier for community colleges than for four-year institutions because the two-year colleges are not burdened with as much of the baggage that often weighs down such ventures.

In North Carolina, community colleges are already actively involved in dealing with school dropouts—a group with which higher education seldom has contact. The National Model Dropout Information and Service Project is operating through nine community colleges that together serve areas including more than 20 school districts. A network has been established by the community colleges to obtain the names of all students within a short time after they drop out of high school. The youngsters are contacted by phone or letter or in person.

A series of options, all run through the community colleges, is presented to the young people. They are told they can enroll in any of the following community college programs:

- High school classes that are limited to adults
- Adult basic education to get their skills up to at least the ninth grade level
- Classes to prepare for the high school diploma by equivalency examination
- Independent study to prepare for the high school diploma by equivalency examination
- A Human Resources Development program to learn the rudiments of how to go about getting a job and how to hold onto a job
- Vocational education for a year or less to gain the skills for a specific job

The City University of New York has also taken an interest in dropouts, starting a program in 1980 at six of its community colleges to help people prepare for the high school equivalency test. The program is run in conjunction with the New York City Board of Education, which pays for the coordinators, teachers, and paraprofessionals. In turn, the university actually does the hiring, training, and supervision of the staff.

Each college at which classes meet is responsible for organizing, promoting and supervising its program. One of the keys to success is the fact that the program operates on college campuses, where the students not only feel a sense of greater self-esteem, but also have access to various college services, including counseling. They also feel comfortable remaining at those campuses for further education after obtaining the diploma.

■ ■ ■ ■ ■ ■ ■ ■ ■ ■ ■ ■ ■ ■ ■ ■ ■ ■

IN THIS FINAL CHAPTER, the emphasis has been on the great variety of programs that can be promoted as selected schools and colleges decide to share facilities, teachers, and resources. The goal should be to agree upon objectives, collaboratively shape a program, and tackle it together. The possibilities of cooperation are limited only by the dedication and imagination of the partners.

The jurisdictional boundaries separating schools and colleges are crossed successfully only when institutions on both sides of the line are amenable. It is not easy to build incentives for cooperation if one institution considers itself the winner and the other sees itself as the loser. Competition does not easily breed cooperation, especially in an area in which so many institutions claim that their survival is at stake.

We return to an essential theme. In all of this, a special burden falls on higher education. The nation's colleges and universities must resist the inclination toward aloofness, and in tangible ways affirm the essentialness of the nation's schools.

NOTES

I. PARTNERSHIP FOR EXCELLENCE

1. Personal Interview.
2. Atkinson, Brooks (Ed.). *Walden and Other Writings of Henry David Thoreau* (New York: Random House, 1950), p. 47.
3. Labaree, Leonard W. *The Papers of Benjamin Franklin*, vol. 4 (New Haven: Yale University Press, 1961), pp. 40-42.

II. SETTING STANDARDS

1. Barry, Paul. "Interview: A Talk with A. Bartlett Giamatti," *College Board Review*, Spring, 1982, p. 7.
2. The Carnegie Foundation for the Advancement of Teaching. *High School*, Forthcoming.
3. President's Commission on Foreign Language and International Studies. *Background Papers and Studies* (Washington, D.C.: U.S. Government Printing Office, November, 1979), p. 10.
4. National Association of Secondary School Principals. *College Admissions: New Requirements by the State Universities* (Reston, Virginia: 1982), p. 4.
5. Ohio Advisory Commission on Articulation Between Secondary Education and Ohio Colleges. *Final Report* (Columbus: Ohio Board of Regents and the State Board of Education, April, 1981), p. 2.
6. *Ibid.*, p. 5.
7. Personal Interview.
8. The Carnegie Foundation for the Advancement of Teaching. *High School*, Forthcoming.
9. California Round Table on Educational Opportunity "Statement of Purpose and Initial Agenda," mimeographed, March, 1981, p. 5.
10. "An Open Letter to High School Students and Their Parents From the University of Utah." *The Salt Lake Tribune*, February 7, 1982, p. 20a.
11. Gardner, David Pierpont. Open letter to members of the University of Utah Institutional Council, June 14, 1982.
12. Western Interstate Commission for Higher Education. *Critical Choices in Western Higher Education: Conference presentation, October, 1981* (Boulder, Colorado: March, 1982), p. 27.

III. ACCELERATING STUDENTS

1. Fund for the Advancement of Education. *They Went to College Early*, Evaluation Report no. 2 (New York: 1957), p. vi.

2. Blackmer, Alan R. *General Education in School and College: A Committee Report by Members of the Faculties of Andover, Exeter, Lawrenceville, Harvard, Princeton, and Yale* (Cambridge, Massachusetts: Harvard University Press, 1952), p. 9.
3. Conversation with Eleanor Dill, Advanced Placement Program, College Entrance Examination Board.
4. Hanson, Harlan P. "Twenty-Five Years of the Advanced Placement Program: Encouraging Able Students." *College Board Review*, Spring, 1980, p. 10.
5. McConnell, Bill. *High School Graduates: Projections for the Fifty States* (Boulder, Colorado: Western Interstate Commission for Higher Education, 1979), p. 31.
6. Wilbur, Franklin P. "High School-College Partnerships Can Work!" *Educational Record*, Spring, 1981, p. 42.
7. *Ibid.*, p. 41.
8. Personal Interview.
9. Personal Interview.

IV. PREPARING TEACHERS

1. Personal Interview.
2. Personal Interview.
3. Personal Interview.
4. Personal Interview.
5. Personal Interview.
6. Personal Interview.
7. Correspondence with the author, July 7, 1982.
8. Commission on the Humanities. *The Humanities in American Life* (Berkeley: University of California Press, 1980), p. 56.
9. Personal Interview.
10. Personal Interview.
11. Personal Interview.
12. Personal Interview.
13. Personal Interview.
14. Personal Interview.

V. BLENDS: EXPERIMENTS IN TRANSITION

1. Hutchins, Robert Maynard. *The Higher Learning in America* (New Haven: Storrs Lectures, Yale University Press, 1936), p. 91.
2. For more on Pasadena Junior College see Whitlock, Baird W. *Don't Hold Them Back: A Critique and Guide to New High School-College Articulation Models* (New York: College Entrance Examination Board, 1978).
3. Handelman, Eileen T. *Profile of Simon's Rock of Bard College*. Prepared for the U.S. Department of Education, National Commission on Excellence in Education, mimeographed, undated (circa June, 1982) p. 3.
4. The Carnegie Commission on Higher Education. *Less Time, More Options: Education Beyond the High School* (New York: McGraw-Hill, 1971); *Continuity and Discontinuity: Higher Education and the Schools* (New York: McGraw-Hill, 1973).
5. Personal Interview.

6. Greenberg, Arthur and Lieberman, Janet. "High-Risk Students Make Big Gains," *Synergist*, Winter, 1981, p. 7.
7. Personal Interview.

VI. MINORITIES: A SHARED MANDATE

1. Personal Interview.
2. Hentoff, Nat. "Profiles: The Integrationist," *The New Yorker*, August 23, 1982, p. 71.
3. California Round Table on Educational Opportunity. Statement of Purpose and Initial Agenda presented at first meeting of the Round Table, mimeographed, March, 1981, pp. 2-3.
4. "Minorities in Engineering," *Engineering Manpower Bulletin* No. 53, January, 1982, p. 1, 3.
5. Personal Interview.
6. Guralnick, S. A. and Schug, K., Chicago Area Health and Medical Careers Program; Second Interim Report, mimeographed, December, 1981, p. 13.
7. McDonald, Kim. "Medical Schools Fear U.S. Cuts Will Hurt Blacks," *The Chronicle of Higher Education*, November 17, 1982, p. 1.
8. Minorities in Medicine: draft of the report of a conference sponsored by the Robert Wood Johnson Foundation, Josiah Macy, Jr., Foundation, and Exxon Education Foundation, November 19-20, 1981, p. 10.

VII. SPECIAL MODELS

1. Personal Interview.
2. Address by John Brademas at the opening session of the National Forum and Annual Business Meeting of the College Entrance Examination Board in New York, New York, October 25, 1982.

INDEX

79